THINK Z

HOW I STARTED AND SOLD MY BUSINESS THE GEN Z WAY

BRANDON AMOROSO

INTRO TO BRANDON

Brandon Amoroso is the founder and President of Shopify Plus agency Electriq. He built the agency to oversee more than 55 brands and 45 team members in just three years before DRINKS.com acquired it in April 2022. Under Brandon's leadership, Electriq achieved the highest certifications available for the DTC industry, including Shopify Plus, Klaviyo Elite, Attentive Pioneer, Okendo Platinum, and more, including the exclusive Recharge Agency Partner of the Year award. Brandon's model has successfully scaled early-stage start-ups, Fortune 1000 companies, and everything in between.

Since the acquisition, he has continued to run the agency while overseeing DRINKS' strategic partnership with Shopify and the DRINKS App, the world's first real-time alcohol tax and compliance solution integrated natively into Shopify's checkout.

Brandon is a thought leader in the ecommerce, beverage alcohol, and entrepreneurship space, writing a weekly newsletter with 10,000+ subscribers, hosting two podcasts, the D2Z Podcast and DRINKS.com podcast, creating long-form YouTube tutorial walkthroughs for aspiring business owners, and more.

As a Gen Z entrepreneur, Brandon's business approach focuses on creating empowered and thriving teams as a key driver of business success. His entrepreneurial endeavors work to break the mold and develop innovation for clients and their customers. His book, *Think Z*, will be published later this year and is meant to serve as a framework for other Gen Z entrepreneurs to use as they pursue their own entrepreneurial endeavors.

Above all, Brandon is passionate about building businesses in industries that are rife with inefficiencies and legacy biases and processes. His new startup, SCALIS, was cofounded last year with his brother Parker, a recent graduate of Stanford, after Brandon's frustrations with the hiring process, difficulty finding qualified and diverse talent, and Parker's experience applying for internships. SCALIS is the world's first fully integrated job board and ATS platform, leveraging AI and machine learning to democratize hiring by matching relevant candidates with relevant employers. The product will be publicly available in September of this year, and they are in the process of closing their seed round now.

WHERE IT STARTS

I'M A FIVE-YEAR-OLD BOY STANDING ON THE FACTORY FLOOR OF my dad's alcohol business. Bottles move along conveyors in perfect automation. Workers pack and tape boxes. Pallets are stacked. Trucks are loaded. Each one of those bottles will end up in a logistics and fulfillment whirlwind before it arrives at someone's doorstep. And that someone will open the bottle and drink from it. A person I never met before. A person I will never know.

Even at five, that was a magnificent thought.

The promise of entrepreneurship was always in my family. My father started companies when I was a kid, and my youngest memories resonate with the constant flutter of business. I grew up in warehouses watching shipments come and go. It was infatuating. I would just stand there and take it all in. The scale of it. The energy of it.

I wanted to do that. Not necessarily food or beverage, bottling, brewing, distribution, or logistics, but business; I wanted to do business. For me, the thrill of building, owning, and growing something was what drew me in. That was infused in my being on those factory floors.

When I was older, the desire to build something of my own was transformed from a slight predisposition into a life dream and goal. I witnessed a close family friend start, scale, and sell a technology company, only to throw himself into multiple other entrepreneurial endeavors. He had what you'd expect a SoCal entrepreneur to have. The cars, the house–the whole thing. I met him for the first time when I was seven and then started visiting him and his family when I was 11 or 12, and while I can't speak for him, I'm sure he knew me as the wide-eyed kid who was always shocked and impressed by everything he did.

I was! It was hard to imagine how someone would want to live any other way.

Sure, the material objects that come with being a successful entrepreneur are nice, and as a kid, that was some of the allure. But as I got older, I saw the immense gratification and excitement that building a business can bring and the responsibility you take for all your team members to keep the business running and thriving.

I started working at his company while in high school. I got a taste of startup life for the first time as a social media intern. Indirectly, I started a course on what would become my entrepreneurship fast track.

My day-to-day was the marketing track, but I was working full-time in a growing company involved in every aspect. I got to sit in on venture capital firm and investor calls, prep for board meetings, and see P&L models be built, things I really had no business being a part of at 19 or 20 years old. I was intimately involved with basically everything it took to grow a company. All of this while I was still in college.

Tuesdays were the worst.

I would start at 8 am. I would take Bella, my puppy at the time, with me to class until 12:30. Bella and I had playtime for an hour, then we'd go back to class until 9:20 pm. I did this on Thursdays too, but only until 6:30 pm. All so I could attend classes two days a week and work three days a week and an occasional weekend.

It wasn't about marketing or the job–that was just the field I was learning. It was about the business of business. It was about making something from nothing and growing it.

This is how it begins. Every entrepreneur has a similar story. There is a captivation for the potential of things. A mentor–or an army of them–bringing them into the movement. The insatiable desire to build.

The origins of entrepreneurs are timeless. My journey is no different than countless others that build our world day after day. And they tirelessly create what will become their future.

Here is where my story diverges from some of the others you've heard. I've only ever built businesses, and I've only ever done it in one of the most disruptive and unpredictable times in modern history.

I'm a Gen Z entrepreneur (according to people who like labels). I entered a space, in this case, the Shopify ecosystem, with no institutional learning, generational baggage, or prescription for how things should be done.

What I did have was the freedom to do what I wanted, the mentorship of people I trusted, a supportive mom, and an infatuation with the concept of building businesses.

Does that make me special? Bella probably thinks so, but that's not my place to say. What I can say is that I have a fresh perspective and have managed to forge a new way with that perspective.

I sincerely believe it's time for the business world to adapt to a new way of thinking rooted in the ability to think outside the box, break down corporate hierarchy, and allow for quick and iterative pivots.

They call Gen Z digital natives, but the truth is it's more than that. We are natives of disruption. We have only ever known a world in flux, so we're uniquely positioned to navigate that world.

My journey is the best way I have to communicate that. Taking this journey with me means opening your mind to new perspectives and focusing on the human experience as your fundamental goal. Together, we will talk through what we can learn from my experience and look at building our businesses to create the world we want.

This isn't meant to be an autobiography or prescriptive rhetoric on how you need to build a business. Instead, I set out to write this book so that each chapter has takeaways and ideas for those on their own entrepreneurial journey, using the 4-year start, scale, and sale of my company, Electriq Marketing, as a guide. I created this book focusing on what I could have benefited from knowing on day one at Electriq.

THE GEN Z ENTREPRENEUR

Day to day, I don't believe younger entrepreneurs are all that different from any other entrepreneur. We are focused on the same things:

1. We want a thriving business.

2. We want the company to grow.

3. We want our people to be valuable team members.

4. We want our business to be successful.

A note on success: Success is not a one-size-fits-all equation. What success looks like is entirely personal. Success for one person is different from what it looks like for another. It's essential to define what success looks like for you and then have that communicated throughout your organization.

I could scale my business effectively because I had business mentors who helped me with everything from employment contracts to organizational structure and process development. I learned from them what makes companies valuable and how to build repeatable and scalable processes. That was an essential part of getting me to where I am.

And I had family support. My brother, Parker, jumped in to help with SEO and content marketing while my mom came on full-time to handle HR and payroll, using her maiden name so the team wouldn't know she was my mom!

But it's just the beginning. There's so much more left to be done now that my mentors helped me get to this place. I've only been at this for four years now, and considering I just turned 26, the sky's the limit for how I can continue to improve myself, learn from others, invest within the ecosystem, and help others out.

But being a Gen Z entrepreneur, with the understanding I needed to establish wisdom to get to this point, I have a different generational approach to business that is entirely alien to other generations, or at least outside of their business calculus.

The Gen Z difference is not exactly tangible. I'm sure there will be a hundred blog lists over the next few years that say things like "10 Ways Gen Z Entrepreneurs Are Different." I look forward to reading those. They will likely not be written by Gen Z entrepreneurs.

As of writing this book, more about Gen Z entrepreneurs needs to be written. There is plenty about Gen Z in the workplace, and we have things like 30 Under 30, but I'd wager to say that the business world still looks at Millennials as the up-and-comers.

That may be a good thing. Maybe they won't see us coming.

What makes us different? What are our approaches, and how do they contrast traditional business thinking? I can only say what I've done in my short but dramatic journey in entrepreneurship.

A few things are going for us. First, we don't know what we don't know. We are not bound by traditional business thinking simply by default. Unlike prior generations, we are resting on our own observations. We can access whatever information we want at any time and are highly skilled at connecting the dots. So while we listen to mentors and sometimes have formal educations, we've already drawn some of our own conclusions by the time we get there. Prior generations didn't have that kind of access, so they had to rely on the system to find their way, inevitably falling in line with that system.

This truly is the most incredible time in our history for those passionate about learning and disrupting. It has never been easier to access information.

Second, we were born, raised, and came of age in one of the most disruptive times in recent history. I don't mean to discount the Boomers coming of age in the 60s, the Xers with the climax and fall of the Cold War, or Millennials with the War on Terror. Every generation had its significant disruption. But what's different about us is that we were raised in a world with no geographical boundaries, no limit to access to information, a worldwide pandemic and seismic shift in how work is conducted, and a complete toppling of various social conventions–including economic ones.

As a result, we are used to risk and uncertainty. It's sort of our natural habitat. We are completely and totally okay with not knowing how things will turn out and have never known a world where one can feasibly plan ten, five, or even one year ahead.

Finally, the major difference with Gen Z as entrepreneurs is that we are not necessarily profit-motivated. I'm not going to sit here and say it's not important, but our desire is not excessive *Games of Thrones* levels of incomprehensible wealth. We just want financial freedom to have the ability to live and experience life in whatever way we want to live and experience life. But that's the key; wealth isn't the goal–living life to its fullest is.

We are untethered to traditional ways, comfortable with uncertainty, and unmotivated by excessive wealth. Attractive traits for entrepreneurship!

I talk a lot about my generation, not necessarily because I'm speaking to them. On the contrary, I'm speaking with them to other generations. Many of us are unified on several fronts, one of which is that the business world needs to adapt to this new era of uncertainty. They need to shift how they think, manage their culture, and conduct themselves in the marketplace because Gen Z is the start of a wave of generations aligned around this new normal. Being different just for the sake of being different is not a reason to be different.

I don't speak on behalf of Gen Z, certainly not. We don't see eye to eye on everything or even most things. But I can talk as a person with a Gen Z perspective—someone equally eager to learn as he is to teach. Our job as business leaders is to make the world a better place and pave the way for others to make a difference.

THE EIGHT APPROACHES

I'm sure I have a bazillion different approaches than other entrepreneurs. And I'm sure that some of my methods align with non-Gen Z business leaders. But I call out these specific approaches because the rest of the business world does not seem entirely aligned around them. And if they were, things would be much easier for them as the world continues to be the way that it is.

My business approaches were not found academically. So to uncover them, we'll look at different moments in my four-year business-building journey that encapsulated what I learned and how that informed my business leadership going forward.

I aim to pay these learnings forward so that other business leaders can see their value and find ways to improve so they can create an agile and successful business in uncertain and risky times.

An Office Does Not Make a Business

A thriving culture has nothing to do with office space, and neither does the legitimacy of your business.

It's a DTC World

Direct long-term relationships with customers are the way through uncertain times.

Delegation Is Not Optional

We can't do everything, and we shouldn't try.

Iteration is Life

Businesses are organisms, not stationary things.

Team Members Are Partners

Find people better than you at what they do and empower them to own their work from top to bottom.

Build for Scale

Start a business with the understanding it will outgrow you.

It Takes a Village

Partnerships aren't just a marketing strategy.

Exit Strategy

Plan for what comes next.

WHAT LED ME HERE

Looking back at it now, it feels like the journey has gone incredibly quickly. Relative to the rest of my life, it did. But the reality is that I'm currently at the culmination of four years of non-stop, day-in and day-out effort to get to this point.

I left my job in the middle of 2018 to freelance. Just in time for graduation in May 2019, I had grown my book of business enough to hire a full-time employee and officially launch the agency. Fast-forward 18 months of grinding away, and we're a team of 11. That's when things started to accelerate - 2021—beginning with eleven team members and ending the year with 45.

A long burn in the beginning, with meteoric growth at the end. A culmination of relentless outreach, referrals, good work, and case studies. I'm impatient. The journey went slower than I would have liked, but stepping back a bit, the acceleration was staggering.

I don't have all the answers, but I have learned a thing or two. And those eight approaches are the glue that seems to bind all of this together. I'm excited to take you on this journey, and I hope you find all the blunders I made along the way as amusing as I do!

I

AN OFFICE DOES NOT MAKE A BUSINESS

THERE ARE NO WORDS TO DESCRIBE WHAT GOES THROUGH THE mind of a young entrepreneur who takes their first steps into their first office. One may imagine a dramatic moment, eyes glistening with tears of joy. A stoic expression on their face as they take in the experience—the first true milestone of running their own business.

In that mental visual, you may have seen a bright glass-filled office with a cityscape beyond—an open office plan with lots of desks and new computers. You might even have visualized a receptionist's desk. A Keurig. Possibly a yoga ball. A foosball table.

My first office was more like what you would have found on the set of *Breaking Bad*. Think Saul Goodman's first office tucked behind a nail salon. I went back to see if it still exists, and it's gone.

Swelling with joy? Maybe. It was perhaps fear.

It was dingy. There was no natural light. I had to sojourn through an industrial complex to get to it. We were in the back corner. There was no parking, but luckily my tiny LA Chinatown apartment was within walking distance.

If it were the 1920s, we would serve illegal spirits there, which would be super cool.

But I had Wi-Fi and a printer, and Bella (my dog) could come.

It was a glorious milestone.

Until now, I'd found random LA coffee shops (you should try Verve if you haven't been) to be an adequate office. A palatable energy comes from being around other people that helps me focus. And I got out of my apartment. Even if it wasn't a traditional office, it provided a sort of *je ne sais quoi*. At least I wasn't working beside where I slept (thanks, COVID). I was in a physical location dedicated to one purpose. Focus.

And caffeine.

Okay, two purposes.

But now I crossed the threshold. I was an actual business owner. With an office. And employees. Well, employee. Singular.

And then there was a second.

And a third–but she quit in three days because it was too dark. Who could blame her? Though part of me still finds it slightly amusing that she was expecting something better from a 2-person marketing agency with no capital.

But everything was lined up. I'd worked for a year and a half through college in ecommerce marketing, specifically in the wine industry, before taking the leap to freelancing and doing my own thing.

In the beginning, I worked for free or very little to help small merchants. I would build Shopify stores for small mom-and-pop artisans, usually one or two-person companies. I found most of them by attending Renegade Craft Fairs and forcing myself to walk up to their booths and introduce myself, something I was highly uncomfortable with at the time as an introvert. They didn't know what they were doing, and while I didn't know much either, I was learning and willing to take risks to figure it out. I did a lot of testing in a low stakes environment to see what worked and what didn't.

This went on for about a year, and then I graduated. I had offers to go the traditional job path after college that would've paid six figures a year and had me in a much more stable place, but now I was standing in my first office in Chinatown, and there was no turning back.

Nothing was very complicated–it was kind of nice, even if it lacked airflow.

I look back at that moment fondly but also with some wisdom that can only come from going through the journey. Now I understand better what business is, what culture is, and what it means to be a business leader.

And I have to ask ... why? What was driving this need to have a physical office? A place with employees. What did this office have that Starbucks didn't?

Like most in business, I assumed an office provides some officiality. It is a mark of legitimacy. Now instead of doing a hobby that pays for nights out, I had a real business with employees in a real office.

A lot changed in just a few short years. We saw an era of uncertainty triggered by COVID that shows no sign of stopping. My industry went through the roof and then came crashing back down to reality. My business grew beyond my expectations and was even acquired!

It's wild to think it's only four years since I left school, but the journey has been explosive. And as I look back, there's quite a bit I still don't know, but I know for sure that the age-old view that a business constitutes four walls, a bunch of desks, and a 9-5 is not only inaccurate, it is dysfunctional.

That mindset cannot survive the age of uncertainty.

WHAT PROMPTED ALL THIS?

I didn't set out to be a business leader and entrepreneur with Electriq, even though I knew that eventually, I wanted to start and run my own business (I thought that timing would have been substantially further down the road). I primarily monetized my skills to enjoy the finer things in life. So when I started freelancing, there was no pressure. Everything was exciting. I got my first client, launched my first website, and registered a business. No stress whatsoever. I miss those days.

I was still in school, and I had a part-time job. So I was just having fun with no risk. And I was learning so much every single day.

However, I knew I would have to do something at some point. After all, I had to graduate eventually! Could I do this full-time? Or would I have to do the impossible?

Get a real job.

I played in the "real job" arena. I saw that I would be in a not exciting or challenging role and it would not provide the level of responsibility and autonomy I sought. I need to be a real contributor, not just a cog in a machine.

Speaking of hiring and finding a job being a nightmare... check out what I'm working on now at SCALIS.ai.

Plus–the interview process. Ugh. Picturing myself going to interview upon interview, finding a good company, and making sure they will allow me to thrive and not pigeonhole me based on my experience—just a nightmare for me.

In today's job market, youth plays against you. Even if you are hired for your tenacity, you are put in a box with few responsibilities. I wanted to create tangible results and impact my daily life. Fundamentally, I was ready for far more than any company could have offered me.

So for me, there was little choice.

I didn't go down the typical post-grad track. You wouldn't find me at any career fair or networking event, though; Don't tell my mother that! I didn't bother with the investment banking or management consulting career fairs. It just wasn't enjoyable.

But my laissez-faire approach to post-grad life mainly concerned me because I didn't know what I wanted to do if I were to start something on my own.

If I just woke up one day and birthed a business entity, I had no idea what to do with it.

But I had a small freelancing business and was pulling in some money. So… what was next? Was I serious about this, or was it just a phase to get me through school?

Did I know what the hell I was doing?

I did everything on my own. I had no sounding board; having a founding team would have been very beneficial. As it happens, I had mentors who helped me through the thick of it and pushed me to take the leap, which I don't think I could have done without.

But here I was—I'd done it. I turned down the secure job offer and leaped (something my dad was even hesitant about). I had my dingy office. I had my first employees. I had my business.

There's never a better time to start your business than when you're young with no real responsibilities.

SO, HAVE YOU EVER STARTED A BUSINESS RIGHT BEFORE A GLOBAL PANDEMIC?

I don't think I'm alone when I say I didn't expect 2020. At that time, I was just finding my direction. Well, more than that… I needed clients. So, there I was cold outreaching prospects from my school email (I did this because it bypassed spam filters–pro tip for all you college entrepreneurs!)

I went the extra mile. I sent over 150 boxes of wine with handwritten letters to CEOs of companies I could only ever dream of working with, simply asking for 15-30 minutes of their time. It was hard work, but I'm confident they would have never spoken to me if I didn't put in that effort. Nothing is more surreal than seeing some of them just a few years later at conferences where I'm presenting keynotes.

Initially, I was willing and able to offer my services for free or extremely cheap. I mean really, really cheap. I remember when I closed my first $150/mo client, and I was pumped. I did that to build up a catalog of work, case studies, and client reviews. I knew even at that stage I'd need proof I was worth hiring, especially as I tried to work my way upmarket. I also had the luxury to do this while I was a student and part-time employed.

Beyond the cold outreach, I also physically went to craft fair shows in and around the LA area, even traveling to a couple to find small artisan makers and merchants who had Shopify stores that needed help. I started generating revenue, building a portfolio of clients, and finally got to the point where I was dealing with headaches like payroll and taxes–a typical entrepreneurial hustle.

Then the pandemic hit just as Electriq started its first massive growth phase. I had a new office and about five employees, and the world changed.

Creating a culture was so much more difficult with remote work. There was no longer constant human interaction with the team, and we lost the natural collaboration that inherently comes from that. And boy, it was a mad dash to revamp and build out processes enabling us to thrive as a company.

Years later, we are virtual first. Everything is handled virtually, whether we're creating messaging and materials or hosting all-team weekly meetings, coming up with new and creative ideas to still foster that community and culture despite us not being in person.

Frankly, there's no need for a Mon-Fri 9-5 office, though I enjoy having something to break up the monotony of working from home every day, especially in today's remote age. I think it's important to be able to provide somewhere team members can go if they want–like coworking spaces–but it certainly doesn't need to be required. Some people just want to work from home. Businesses should let their team do what makes them most effective. There is no one-size-fits-all approach.

Starting a new business however, like I recently did with SCALIS, I did not and would not go remote first. We are a hybrid work environment, spending 2-3 days a week in the office. Having the founding team of a startup in person is vital for brainstorming, collaboration, and building the culture and foundation that will be the backbone of your business for the rest of the time.

My perspective on needing the traditional Mon-Fri 9-5 office shifted once I realized that I could still have a grasp of and create a robust organizational framework with processes despite everything being remote. And I'm confident it made us better organizationally as it forced us to accelerate this process creation exercise and be extremely tight with following them once they were in place. That being said, we still make time to have in-person company meetings and events because human connection and bonding are important.

COVID was a force function to tighten how we work with clients and handle processes and deliverables.

I still have a personal affinity for offices just because I enjoy that human interaction. But it's not necessary whatsoever in today's world.

The 9-5 Monday through Friday is dead, and I don't see it returning anytime soon.

My Tip: Work on Saturday and Sunday mornings. This might not be for everyone, but I fondly remember by weekend 6 a.m.-11 a.m. San Diego coffee shop work sessions where I could finally enter into a flow state, uninterrupted by Slack, emails, or calls, and solely focused on the weeks and months ahead. By working in the mornings, I could still have a social life, get outdoors, and enjoy non-work activities I loved. It's not an either-or situation.

THE FUNDAMENTAL SHIFT IN WORKFORCE CULTURE

The shift to work from home prompted many changes, but the biggest was a fundamental shift in the workforce's mindset. I have no evidence here, but people started to reflect on their working lives due to the pandemic. Sure, there was the existential dread, but also the empowerment they had over their work. They worked in the way that made them most effective and allowed them time to be a person and handle needs at home.

Managers couldn't stare over their shoulders and tell them what to do at every turn. The minutiae of wasted time (commutes, regular work interruptions, useless meetings) gave them the time and freedom to tackle their work in unprecedented ways.

Sure, there is a cost to this. There are more silos. Collaboration is hard. Culture-building is even more challenging. But these aren't insurmountable, and the benefits can significantly outweigh the issues.

So when companies started announcing return to office plans, we saw an outright revolt in the workforce. First was the Great Resignation and then Quiet Quitting. Lots of pundits have opinions about this, but the fact is the workforce is done with the old way. They are setting boundaries, starting their own gigs, reframing conversations, and outright refusing to do what their bosses say. They even moved to different states and cities.And it seems the more businesses pull out their sledgehammers, the more the workforce resists.

On the one hand, this has divided organizations and is causing huge disruptions. On the other hand, the workforce is trying to take control of their destinies and balance their lives–making them more enriched.

What does the future hold? How will organizations evolve? What is the fallout of all this?

I ACCIDENTALLY FOUND AN ANSWER

When I started the agency, I had zero experience and zero understanding of how other agencies ran. I was not using any pre-existing mindset or frameworks because I had none. I didn't know how agencies operated, worked with clients, or the "best practices."

That allowed me to come in and shake things up a bit and change how things were done, especially from the perspective of building a team. It also made me think we could make do without account managers–we couldn't!

The foundation of my business was ripe with a Gen Z team member base. Whether or not we realized it then, we were cultivating a space for people that would thrive in a post-Great Resignation world. From the beginning, we naturally had the mindset that Gen Z is demanding in other workplaces. We didn't know what we didn't know–so we didn't replicate the system that Gen Z workers are currently retaliating against.

All the processes we've built out with the agency and everything we've done have been the byproduct of raw creativity and problem-solving. And we're not stuck in our ways because we didn't even have ways. We're building them as we go, which for the most part, is positive and very powerful.

I schedule a 15-minute call with every new team member to get to know them, give them the origin story of Electriq, and express who we are and what we do. I'd highly recommend every CEO do this, no matter the size of their business. During this call, I stress to every new team member that Electriq abides by a philosophy of continual improvement. Just because we have a process doesn't mean it can't be made better.

In the beginning, there was no structure, and we were just making it up as we went. Quite literally, every client onboarded had a different onboarding process!

That's also not great either.

Now we're in a place where we have a templated process for working with clients, but it's not rigid. We are comfortable with making changes daily if there's a way that it could be better or would improve how we work, what we do, what we're focusing on, how we're managing our time—whatever it may be.

So we keep that mindset that nothing is perfect, and no one is always right. That allows us to continually improve and thrive with our clients, take in that feedback, and turn it into positive improvements.

> *I've tried to instill this mindset of continual improvement in myself and the team since day one. Just because something has been done this way for a while does NOT mean it's immutable.*

And this mindset is recognized by the ecosystem as well.

So often, I heard from my friends who were going to get "real jobs" that they were going into businesses or corporations with rigid and defined paths and structures for how you grow within the company. Their internal processes were set in stone, and you didn't have the right to have an opinion on how they could improve.

A lot of times, it was you worked three years, had a performance review, and then you either got fired or promoted. And there is the idea that you are not there for your opinions and ideas yet because you are just out of school, so you don't know anything. That's a common attitude of businesses.

And that's one of the things Gen Z is rising up against in the business world. They want the freedom and the trust to own their work, not to be micromanaged and disregarded, and to be treated like professionals from the outset, no matter their experience. They want to be heard.

> *Experience is important, but it's not the end-all-be-all. At Electriq, career growth was based entirely on results. You could have ten years of experience, and your manager could have six months. I'm a strong believer in rewarding merit. This isn't to say that it's a bad thing if you have a lot of experience and report to more "junior" people. Everyone has their own goals, both personally and professionally. It's your job as CEO to understand your team's goals and empower them to achieve them. If everyone wanted to be a CEO, there would be no business!*

It is an injustice to hamper or disregard someone's creativity who is just entering the workforce. And you'd be very surprised at how positively my age group and younger will respond to getting that level of respect and autonomy from the get-go. Certain things need to be earned, and you still have to earn your stripes, but I think we took a completely different approach.

We built an open business in the sense that everybody is expected to bring ideas and strategies to the table and have very strong opinions about what they think would or would not work. No matter if you've worked at the company for a week or three years. No matter if you went to a fancy school or not. No matter if this was your first job or your tenth.

If only a select few people are allowed to speak on strategy, then you'll be missing out on a lot. The worst thing that happens is you take the idea and realize that, hey, maybe this doesn't make sense, or you talk about it, and that's it. The bottom line is that you nurture a culture of ideas, no matter the source, age, gender, color, etc., so that the organization is stronger for it long-term.

SAVE YOUR WORKFORCE BY SHIFTING TO A GEN Z MINDSET

You don't have to be a member of the ubiquitous Generation Z to have a good culture in the workplace. Secondly, Gen Z does not represent some innovation in psychology, nor do we (or anyone else) have all the answers. But what is worth noting is that Gen Z was the first generation to grow up and enter the business world entirely during a time of disruption.

Uncertainty is our normal baseline.

Frankly, if things suddenly became stable and certainty was the norm, I'm not sure how well we'd do. We'd probably get bored (maybe that explains my inability to stay home for more than two weeks).

But that alone means our natural mindset is worth acknowledging and perhaps even adopting. We are inherently nimble and flexible and have an enormous capacity to let water flow under the bridge. It's not because we are amazing (though we might be), but it's because it's our natural posture to be flexible in our uncertain world.

So while we accidentally built a resilient and thriving company simply by being who we are, businesses that are struggling to keep people hired, motivated, or productive could benefit from looking at how we do things.

In general, the organizational model is turned on its head. We value different things. While profit is important, we know that thriving people create a thriving business. So it is every bit as important to our bottom line that our people have the freedom and flexibility to be who they are and work in the way they work as it is for us to land new clients.

Businesses are struggling to keep people during the Great Resignation, perhaps because they don't trust and empower the people they have on board. Why would they stay if folks don't feel like they have a voice or impact in the business? Others may be just phoning it in and quietly quitting because the business has not respected their personal and professional boundaries.

A model built around productivity mandates, micro-management, and selling one's soul to the corporation may have worked well in other business environments over the decades, but in this one, that sort of intransigence can't withstand uncertainty. Companies need to be resilient and flexible, which means their people must be resilient and flexible.

Gen Z may not have the answers, but there is one thing we understand—change and disruption are the new normal. It's only ever been our normal. So the quicker organizations get on board with that idea, the quicker they can grow and thrive.

THE PRACTICAL GEN Z OFFICE

It's all about cultivating the right culture.

Every workplace has a culture, whether they put an emphasis on fostering it into something intentional or not. It is always better to create a strong sense of identity and culture than to have one cultivated without you realizing it.

Fostering this culture is a deliberate act that creates an overall organization aligned with your business vision.

Intentional culture has become even more important as the business world has gone remote. Having a shared sense of identity is more difficult if you do not see your team in person daily. But it's critical to cultivate and foster it despite physical isolation. The team not only needs to keep engaged with the organization, but also the organization needs to attract high-quality team members who thrive on working at a company with a strong identity.

If you know your identity in your culture, you can find better team members that fit within that culture. It becomes much easier to join a team and be a strong fit. That's perhaps an even more significant point. The perils of bringing a person into a team that does not fit with the culture are real.

> *You can teach hard skills to anyone. What can't be taught is culture. I'd rather hire someone with no experience who would fit with our culture, train them for 3-6 months and act as a mentor than hire someone who could contribute deliverables from day one, but that isn't a good fit with the business culture.*

So it is very important to have a strong and defined culture in the workplace. As the company has matured, I'm starting to pay more attention to this. When I started the business, I thought it was maybe more of an afterthought, and I possessed a little bit too much of the "you go to work, you do your job" type of mentality. But when you spend most of your day at your job, ensuring that that culture represents your values and personal purpose is critical.

Culture can be fostered by the collective group as a whole, so it shouldn't be a top-down, directed approach to culture. It's not in the company's best interest for me to sit there and say this is what our culture is and not have the entire team make up what that culture is. This is why it's so critical that your first hires are truly bought into the business because it's with them that you'll start to build this foundation of culture.

It's even more important when everyone is not in the same physical space, providing them with outlets to put in their insights, feedback, and suggestions on what that culture should be and their ideas to foster it in a virtual capacity.

And so even simple things from happy hours to parliamentary meetings so that team members can be more comfortable and familiar with others that aren't in their particular departments.

All of our culture-focused activities came from sourcing feedback from the team and asking them what sort of company they think we are. We need to know what values the team thinks we should elicit and then expand upon that as well.

One of the best things I did at Electriq was to send out a mandatory survey to all forty team members at the time, asking them to share three things we were not doing that we should be doing. I took all 120+ ideas, put them into a PowerPoint, and then presented to the entire team on an hour-long call how we were already addressing, were planning to address, or weren't able to address each idea. This not only gave me a TON of valuable feedback and ideas for the business but having that call going through each idea and talking through it together as a team empowered everyone and made it very clear that this was something we were building together.

THE GEN Z OFFICE IS A SHARED CULTURE?

If culture is the foundation of a thriving business, what is the desired Gen Z culture? I discovered a culture defined from the bottom-up but fueled and supported by the top, creates a shared and intentional culture. But what kind of culture do folks with a Gen Z mindset thrive in?

There are a lot of things one can point to as representative of Gen Z work culture. Bringing dogs to work (Bella is the cursor on our website, after all), taking a hike guilt-free on the weekends without expecting work to creep up, mutual respect, honest communication, and more.

But those are all qualities that stem from one fundamental outlook: trust.

Gen Z culture tends to be built on trust.

Supervisors trust the team to get the job done without breathing down their neck; employers trust employees not to abuse WFH or PTO; team members trust that their supervisors have their back; business leaders trust that their supervisors can manage the business, colleagues trust that other colleagues are adequately qualified for their positions, the organizations trust that everyone has a valid point of view, etc.

As opposed to trust being earned, it's given from day one, starting at Electriq. You're given a high level of autonomy and expectations. However, there is accountability. If you don't deliver, that trust is eroded, and we will find someone who can get the job done.

Modern businesses are largely built around a foundation of distrust. Every process and system is built around edge cases of non-performing employees, dishonest supervisors, and unskilled people in influential positions. While those people or motivations can and do happen in every organization, the Gen Z mindset treats them as the edge cases they are, not the norm. The workplace trusts that people will be and do their best, especially when bought into the company. When they don't, it is dealt with—but not at an organizational level.

This ubiquitous trust empowers teams to take responsibility for their jobs and enables supervisors to lift and support their teams rather than police them. It also relieves business leaders from managing daily because managers can do so.

So while culture shouldn't be created from the top down, the foundations of the culture can. All organizations need to do to cultivate a Gen Z mindset in the workplace is trust their people.

Fool me once, shame on you; fool me twice, shame on me. Trust is essential, and I learned early on that giving people chances to improve is important, but at the same time, there MUST be accountability.

Sometimes you need to rip the Band-Aid off and move on from a team member because it's not working. And more often than not, I found that these team members agreed they weren't happy, were interested in other career opportunities, or something else. You need to be comfortable with having these difficult conversations.

WHY THIS APPROACH WORKS

Folks that are following business trends are seeing this already. A recent Gallup Poll revealed that the number one thing younger workers want is for employers to be concerned about their wellbeing. That same poll said they want their leaders to be ethical. They want inclusivity, diversity, and transparency. Compensation didn't even make the list. Neither did an office with amazing amenities.

I know some legacy thinking out there feeds the idea employers shouldn't really care what employees want. They are there to do a job and nothing else—that their role is to fulfill job requirements, not to be happy.

Let's take a step back. If that's your position, just listen to yourself for a moment. Your team members will likely spend more time with you during an average week than with their families. While work is not life, a good portion of life takes place at work. Do you really want your team to be miserable, under pressure, or stressed for the majority of their time? How helpful, supportive, or productive do you think they'll be?

For those of you that are bottom-line focused (trust me, I get it), let's take empathy out of it. Studies have shown that happy people are 13% more productive. Also, business leaders well know the cost of onboarding folks. Voluntary Turnover and onboarding costs U.S. businesses a trillion dollars every year. An average business will lose $2.5 million per year to this. And that statistic was before the Great

Resignation. Research estimates that the Great Resignation increased turnover by 20%--and it shows no sign of stopping.

Employee retention was one of the most important metrics I tracked and how I gauged my own performance as a leader. Part of the reason we were able to grow so quickly and be successful is we weren't churning through new team members every month. Our badass leadership team hired amazing people who got shit done and bought into the company's vision.

Can it be that voluntary turnover has something more to it than just "people don't want to work anymore?"

The biggest driver (despite what people will tell you if you ask) is compensation. People don't feel like they are paid what they are worth. But surprisingly, there are two other drivers nearly as statistically significant as compensation: "no opportunity for advancement" and "felt disrespected at work." Not too far down the list after that are "insufficient flexibility to choose hours" and "working too many hours."

The data tells a distinct story directly impacting businesses' health, welfare, and profitability. Businesses that thrive consist of people who thrive.

That is why culture is so influential. That is why I managed to grow my company from nothing to more than 45 employees and a successful exit amid the Great Resignation. The Gen Z mindset isn't just about being mouthy and demanding in the workplace. It is about setting actual human boundaries and respecting them so we can all be happier, more productive, and collectively more successful.

A Gen Z mindset doesn't mean you don't want to be successful or are lazy. It's the complete opposite. We're a generation of self-starters who see through the corporate bullshit and know what we're worth. We can be successful without succumbing to a grinding 9-5 corporate life where you're a robot. We probably work longer hours and get more shit done because we are passionate and bought in.

WHAT YOU CAN DO

Earlier in the book, I mentioned this as an aside, but one of the best things I ever did was ask every team member to send me three things they thought we should be doing that we weren't doing—all forty team members.

This was invaluable.

Not only did I get buy-in from the team that they were genuinely building this business along with myself, but it gave me invaluable insight into the day-to-day of our team members, from operational level management down to the interns.

And this gave me a strong sense of where we could optimize and do better–including areas I was falling short of. I then set up a presentation where we went through each item step by step and spoke about how I was addressing each item, or if I wasn't handling it, I explained why.

That level of visibility was powerful. There was just so much team buy-in. Not only did we ask for feedback as an organization, but we acted on it.

People loved it. And for the business, it was invaluable to know what direction the collective thought we should be heading.

The collective thinking power of all forty of our very creative, intelligent, talented team members merged into this beautiful list of 120 suggestions on things we could implement to make ourselves more effective. And it paid off in spades with all of our clients.

You need to source feedback from your team because it's valuable. And if you think it isn't, then maybe they aren't the right fit for the open culture you are trying to build and should bring on team members that will empower your business and the people they work with.

Client and customer feedback is also essential but should be taken with a grain of salt. They have their best interest in mind, which may or may not align with your company's best interests.

That's the first step. Just listen to your people. Find out what they need. And instead of a knee-jerk reaction, reflect on the desired outcome. Are you working to make your business a safe and healthy place for them, or are you pushing them away? Are you cultivating a culture of thriving people, or are you creating undo pressure?

Be honest with yourself and listen to your people and that alone will make your business more resilient as we weather storms like the Great Resignation.

2
IT'S A DTC WORLD

PRIL 26, 2021, WAS NATIONAL PRETZEL DAY. THE OS-CARS HAD just wrapped–late for the season (because of COVID). There was some buzz around it. Perhaps most alarmingly, Bindi Irwin, the grown daughter of legend Steve Irwin, gave her daughter her first pair of Crocodile Hunter kha-kis. Indeed a moment to remember.

I don't remember any of that. Apple's iOS 14.5 update dropped.

The only thing I can tell you about April 26, 2021, was the one singular thought lingering: "Well, this changes things."

Those of you in the e-commerce space would remember this well. For the rest of you, there might be a faint recollection of Mark Zuck-erberg getting mad at Apple for some reason.

The DTC world–well, we were hard at work as always. But we were also in a stasis of waiting. Some of us may be holding our breath too long. We were about to witness the effects of an industry that could no longer rely on Facebook to acquire new customers.

This fight between Apple and Facebook went back several months–maybe longer. And it wasn't much of a battle as it was Facebook grandstanding against a foe they assumed we would all rally against. It was all very one-sided. Apple, they were standing for user privacy. They could care less about Zuck and his stock price.

So what was iOS 14.5 all about?

It was a boring update. It allowed users to unlock their iPhones with their Apple Watch (useful during our masking days). You could now report accidents on Apple Maps. There was a new emoji introduced (hello heart on fire!)

But those weren't the updates Facebook was upset about.

Apple iPhones were now asking people for their consent to have their online activity tracked.

This launched a long and intensive campaign by Facebook against this. But according to Apple's Tim Cook, this was done because "privacy is a fundamental human right."

That's a hard argument to make a stand against, but Facebook did. They bought ads slamming Apple against small businesses, went on media tours, rallied pundits, and did everything they could to change the tide of public opinion.

Ultimately they failed to do so. And on that fateful day, everything changed. Except that it didn't.

> *The ironic part about this whole thing is I predict Apple will sell ads in the not-so-distant future.*

SO WHAT'S THE BIG DEAL?

The cost of acquiring new customers increased long before iOS 14.5 was released. In many ways, the iOS 14.5 "crisis" was a portrait symbolizing a much bigger and wider spread trend. 65% of consumers didn't trust advertising, and 71% didn't trust sponsored ads on social media, before iOS 14.5. The cost of customer acquisition increased by 60% over the past five years. The onset of COVID sent a record number of businesses and entrepreneurs rushing to open their online stores, driving competition to unseen levels.

iOS 14.5 may have been the straw that broke the camel's back, but it just poured fire onto four underlying shifts that were taking place:

More Competition. The onset of COVID sent a record number of businesses and entrepreneurs rushing to open their online stores, driving competition to unseen levels.

Less Customer Demand. As COVID restrictions lifted, consumers craved in-person shopping experiences and returned in full force to traditional retail channels.

Inflation. Customers became tighter and tighter with their wallets, specifically on non-essential items you'd usually find advertised on Facebook.

Investment Shrinkage. Valuations started falling, interest rates rose, and investors got tighter with their money.

In short, the cost of advertising was going to rise either way. More competition for the ad space, fewer eyeballs on the ads, inflation, and less money for marketing were a quadruple whammy. iOS 14.5 amplified the issue by making ads significantly less effective at targeting.

E-commerce relied heavily on Facebook because it had an extensive data bank that allowed them to target with precision and get its message in front of the exact right person. Why invest in other channels when you have a tried and true solution with an advertising platform that you could easily predict the ROI you'd get? When that went away, Facebook's usefulness went away. But Facebook relied on questionable data collection methods to keep their acquisition costs low.

Facebook knew what we all knew; if it costs too much to acquire a new customer, then advertisers go away.

This is the pinnacle of an already devastating trend for advertisers, especially e-commerce, who rely heavily on granular targeting to acquire new customers on an ongoing basis. In many ways, e-commerce is the frontline of the customer acquisition battle, and if you want to know how to succeed in other marketing efforts, look at what e-commerce is doing.

SO WHAT DO WE DO?

How do you get new business in a world where there is too much competition for your audience's attention?

Innovative brands are looking to invest in cracking this problem as they realize that this type of funnel is starting to shrink. Creativity beyond the pulse of what's new and constantly innovating will be rewarded in this space. Because when there are big changes like iOS, for example, there are opportunities for those willing to innovate and jump into new ideas and spaces.

While any change is scary, those who can adapt have outsized opportunities.

Consumers aren't going to be consuming less. Businesses aren't going to stop needing services from other companies. We need to find our audience in different places than before, and brands will need to learn how to innovate.

WHAT INNOVATION LOOKS LIKE

In short, this is the time to throw away everything we thought we knew about marketing. It was built on a more than a hundred-year-old chassis and presupposed principles that are no longer true. In a world where anyone can access anything with a simple scroll of their finger, we cannot rely on traditional advertising and marketing to be effective or even affordable.

Innovation and a new way of thinking have been forced onto e-commerce and DTC brands. We are learning about the importance of automation and technology solutions and the power of focusing a business strategy on keeping customers rather than just trying to obtain new ones. Innovation isn't simply about finding the right tech or using the latest SaaS solutions. It is about adjusting the business mindset to match the environment. Understand how and why the marketplace is shifting and have the flexibility to change with it.

It is about shifting strategies from spending to acquire new customers to innovating systems and processes so that you keep the customers you have. In a word, retention.

THE FUNDAMENTAL PROBLEM

Ultimately, people don't care about your business, product, or service. I mean, not at first. It's easy to forget this, especially on the heels of highly targeted and effective Facebook ads. DTC was going through a veritable golden age because Facebook's extensive data bank allowed marketers to target with a surgeon's precision. They knew they were getting the right person, so acquiring customers costs far less.

For example, you could start and scale a DTC brand that sold sugar-free, paleo pancake mix to a hyper-targeted audience of health-conscious moms to over $50M in revenue from Facebook ads. Starting a brand with such a specific niche would've been encouraged.

But Facebook's database fell under scrutiny. Now, you just can't reach this specific audience with the same precision, making your cost per acquisition prohibitive. Ignoring whether or not their data collection practices were questionable and whether or not you believe iOS 14.5 should have been implemented, isn't that a signal about how far off acquisition strategies are if one platform goes to shit and your business goes with it? Shouldn't we ask ourselves as brands why we rely on one channel to get customers?

DTC managed to survive iOS 14.5, but not without some casualties. The industry was saved due to the pandemic, which drove DTC into record highs before flattening out in 2021. But now we are in a new era. We no longer have cheap acquisition sources we can just flip on. We are at a juncture where we need to acknowledge acquisition strategies of the past are old and tired. How many brands were doing the same thing before consumers got fed up?

Consumers are cynical now. They have strong values. What's more, they have access to all human knowledge in their pockets. They are expensive to acquire–perhaps more costly than the widget you are selling them.

To survive in this climate, you need to break down the preconceptions of old marketing and look at things with a new mindset. Good business, whether it is DTC or something else, is about relationships. Consumers want that, and, in fact, demand it.

Everything else is just noise.

HOW I LANDED ON THE REALITY OF DTC

When I got into this business during and right after high school, I didn't know what I didn't know. I didn't have many of the assumptions clouding the marketplace around acquisition best practices, sales funnels, marketing, or any of it. I just went in with the desired outcome, learned the systems, and saw what worked and what didn't.

There is a lot of legacy thinking that can hold brands back. Remember, this is an era of uncertainty. So, if it worked one month, it probably won't in another. Many brands and agencies don't think like this yet. For someone with no context to come in and look at the environment, there wasn't anything in my mind except what I saw at the moment. I didn't have context or history. I just had the environment.

I used this to my advantage. When questioned about my experience, my common retort was, "Why are you so dead set on working with someone with ten years of email marketing experience when email marketing is changing daily?"

But that right there is the mind shift I'm talking about. If more brands thought about sales and marketing in the context of the environment, staying at the cutting edge of new trends and technology, and not with past successes, things would become much clearer.

If you are focused on the environment (or the marketplace or your customers), then you start creating acquisition funnels and retention programs around what customers want. It will start driving everything from the product to how you communicate. And when you get to that place, customers will genuinely love what you are offering and want to share it and advocate for your brand to all of their friends.

You need to think through how you can take a more organic grassroots approach to growth instead of raising some money and lighting it all on fire on Facebook ads.

I learned this by necessity. When I got into freelancing, Facebook was already a thorn in acquisition. I could tell from the environment that people avoided offers and messages, so acquisition costs were higher. My clients could not afford acquisition (neither could I), so I had to find another way. And that way was simply to listen to what people did want.

The secret to e-commerce is to dive in and start to learn. Endless content on YouTube, Google, and help articles allows you to pick up almost anything and run with it.

You can learn anything on the internet. I logged into a Klaviyo account for the first time in Q3 of 2020. I didn't have a clue how to do email marketing. I had such little experience that Klaviyo's inbound agency partner team even marked Electriq as "not having significant potential." Fast forward to today, we're one of 24 Klaviyo Elite Partners worldwide.

There is no degree for this. No handbook. And any handbook is probably out of date by the time it is published (yes, I do find that I'm publishing a book with this sentence in it pretty contradictory). And that's why I decided to write this book more around processes, mindset frameworks, and things that will stand up more to the test of time. It is about jumping in, examining the landscape, and trying things. It is also about listening and identifying what works and what doesn't. In this era of uncertainty, you can't lock yourself into one way of doing things.

The key to e-commerce today is personalization. It's something that retail can't match for the most part, so you need to lean into that and use it to your advantage across your email and SMS communications and through the website experience.

Start aggregating your zero and first-party data to allow you to personalize better and tailor the customer experience pre- and post-purchase. It will differentiate you from your brand presence in retail and all the competition. For those in retail wondering why to go online? Connection and personalization.

There will be a lot of consolidation and a few players that don't make it in the direct-to-consumer space because of the struggles that brands are having with acquiring customers. Brands need help to hit their revenue projections. I've seen firsthand three brands go under. And in light of the COVID-prompted e-commerce boom, the new players are already unclear why they can't maintain that initial spike. Their expectations and their valuations were unrealistic, given the market conditions.

And it's not just on the brand side either. Technology companies are feeling the impact of all these factors as well.

All this leads to consolidation, and some won't make it.

But those focused on personalization and tailoring the experience to the customer will be in a much stronger position.

The acquisition isn't over. There will be some new players in the space to replace Facebook ads, but they may not be in places you'd expect. I'm looking forward to seeing how Shopify makes an entrance into the media and advertising side of things, given their vast amount of data and need to help their merchants grow. For example, they could easily power a marketplace that surfaces new brands and targets new customers based on their historical information on Shopify brand customers (hello Shop App). A DTC-grown advertising platform could rival Facebook's prior ability to target consumers.

LET'S TALK ABOUT TIMELESS STRATEGIES

But here's the thing. The trends and projections about the marketplace don't matter. If we've learned one thing, change is the only constant. Everything else is variable. So our new mindset needs to be around resiliency, particularly leaning on timeless strategies. That exists no matter what is going on in the world.

That is why I focus on customer relationships as a critical strategy driver. Retention will NEVER go out of style.

One significant component of this new era begins with DTC as a concept. DTC is the business model of the new generation. Companies and even industries that never had a reason to go direct are now doing so en masse. We are seeing everyone from legacy athletic wear to Consumer Packaged Goods. And that is a trend that is not going anywhere.

Why?

Some of this (well, a lot of it) resulted from the pandemic. The industry boomed and is now in a period of resetting. But this industry was growing regardless. The pandemic just sent it into overdrive. And while the initial flash happened and then stabilized, and we saw many problems, such as supply chain issues, the overall trend is here to stay.

Technology has enabled us to exist in a global economy without borders, boundaries, or limits to scale. Brands have little reason to use distributors or intermediaries when they can go directly to the market. And to add to that, the platforms that defined marketing for more than a decade, such as Facebook and Google, are unnecessary gatekeepers that keep brands away from their customers.

DTC solves both systemic problems. Brands can go directly to their customer without worrying about margins and markup. Also, perhaps more importantly, they can cultivate strong relationships directly with their customer, so they don't have to worry about Facebook (or whomever else) having the keys to that relationship. Brands can create their communities. Communities endure many market changes, uncertainty, or acquisition strategy shifts.

Owning one's channel is a resilience strategy. DTC enables that strategy to be possible.

The other component to thriving in an era of certainty is, as eluded to above, establishing relationships and communities. Acquisition strategies have forced us to look at metrics around getting the most amount of people to see and hear your message so the minuscule conversion rate will kick in. It was always a numbers game. If I spend X, then I get Y customers. For too long now, X was less than Y, but now that the equation has become imbalanced, brands can't survive.

That is why relationships matter now more than ever before. It was always true that customer loyalty was a hallmark of good business, but now it's table stakes. If customers are not loyal to you and you are forced to rely on acquisition, you are fighting a losing battle. Additionally, garnering customer loyalty is the only way to make a single customer more valuable. If your widget costs $10 and it's $20 to acquire that customer, you better have them as a customer at least two times.

Customer Lifetime Value (CLTV) has always been the key metric for a thriving business, but the days of brands being propped up by cheap acquisition costs even with poor CLTV are gone.

Acquisition and conversion, while initially important, only tell part of the story. CLTV tells you if your company will thrive or if it will sink.

Would you rather invest in a company that acquires a customer for $50 and spends $200 or a company that acquires a customer for $60 and spends $300?

The timeless strategy that will help you succeed in uncertain times and make your company resilient? Go directly to your customer and build relationships with them. That's it. That's the secret sauce. This is true if you are a shoe manufacturer or an accountant.

Focus on email, SMS, push, and direct mail—all channels where you directly own the relationship with the customer.

WHAT DOES CLTV LOOK LIKE

In the e-commerce space, CLTV is one of many standard metrics. In general, we are tracking the value of a customer for their whole experience with you. In particular, this often refers to business models that are designed around retaining customers month after month.

Acquisition costs aren't impactful if you can pay dividends over a customer's life.

However, this approach works in almost every part of business, not just DTC. For example, if you manage to keep a subscriber from billing cycle to billing cycle, your profitability goes up if you are a service provider. Likewise, retaining clients is far more profitable than acquiring new ones if you are in professional services.

Lifetime Value is also not a new metric. It has been a good business hallmark far before I stepped into it.

But it's not as sexy to say, "We kept 10,000 customers" versus, "We acquired 10,000 new customers!" Working in the trenches with clients going through this colossal era of uncertainty, I've discovered that CLTV is the only metric that counts.

So what does that mean in practice? In short, the best way to keep customers coming back is to treat them well.

Not to sound too obvious, but treating customers well is only sometimes a part of a marketing strategy. And there are layers to that. What does it mean to treat a customer well? Sure, it means treating them how you would be expected to be treated. But there are actionable and measurable ways to do that.

First, companies that shift from a "selling" position to a "helping" position automatically treat customers well. Now they are focused on ensuring the customer has what they need and are not just considered a one-off commodity. People don't want to have transactional experiences. They want to be treated as if they matter and are more than a number. So being helpful is a big step in that direction.

Being helpful doesn't only mean providing resources for customers or education. It certainly can. But it also means making their user experience easy. It means giving them all kinds of levers they can pull to handle their relationship with you. Can customers change their order via text? Can they get an immediate response when submitting a help request via chat? Is the checkout flow simple and quick? Is it easy to find the products they are looking for?

All of these considerations are done in the spirit of helping the customer out. Do you want their experience to be pain-free, easy, and dare I say, fun?

Helping also means using their time effectively. It means serving up what they are looking for when they are looking for it. This is done through personalization.

When people talk about personalization, they mean adding a person's name to an email for a newsletter. But that is a very surface way of looking at it. Personalization is about understanding customers' wants and offering them what is relevant. This means acquiring data about them so you know what products or services relate to them, then giving them ready and easy access to it.

A CLTV-focused strategy is about creating a helpful, welcoming, and easy experience for customers. That experience should be consistent through every interaction they have and explicitly value their needs.

Marketing and communications are then devoted to helping, not selling. Sure, selling happens inherently, and that is the ultimate goal—but the real substance of the content and experience is to make sure the customers are valued. They will take it to heart and stick around.

This model isn't just for e-commerce. It works for all types of businesses and industries. It works for life. If you are a helpful resource and create an accessible and welcoming experience, people will always return to you.

THE DATA

The proof is, as they say, in the pudding.

Let's take a cold, hard look at what's going on with consumer behavior so we can see how shifting to a DTC mindset is helpful in the face of uncertainty.

First, let's acknowledge that consumers, and by extension, people in general, expect options. They expect to have things the way they want them when they want them. We can accept that in the abstract, but what do the numbers say?

Recent data shows that consumers want more payment choices, everything delivered, things to be ethical and sustainable, and perhaps they want a partridge in a pear tree. We might view this as an entitled consumer that believes in the "customer is always right" philosophy. But I think that's not entirely accurate.

You have a supercomputer in your pocket—the summit of human ingenuity. You and basically everyone else on the planet can find anything they want, whenever they want it. We have infinite choices at our disposal. There are no longer geographical boundaries. With all that information and these options, we need a way to filter the noise.

So we go directly to companies and brands that can give us exactly what we want. Why wouldn't we? Why would we waste time on anything else?

Second, we go to brands that share our values.

Of course, we do. Why would we go with someone who doesn't deliver what we want and doesn't see things the way we do? We have infinite choices here. This isn't 1992 when we have three options for coffee. There are hundreds and hundreds of coffee brands if not thousands.

That is why DTC is so important. The best way to demonstrate our values and to provide what our customers want is to have an uninterrupted direct relationship with them.

Increasingly the platforms we rely on to reach our audiences are breaking apart. Facebook's debacle with iOS is just one example. Big box stores are responding by turning toward services and by trying to insert themselves into the e-commerce world–some are doing so quite successfully. But they may not survive this new era if they don't figure out how to adapt to the direct and personal experience customers expect. The supply chain crisis has already cast light on this issue.

Consumers are increasingly adopting an omnichannel approach to shopping, seamlessly transitioning between physical stores, e-commerce websites, and social media platforms to find the best products and deals. Businesses must adopt a holistic approach that prioritizes being present on all these channels while maintaining a laser-focused emphasis on delivering exceptional customer experiences that are integrated cross-channel to stay ahead of the curve. This emphasis is vital in driving customer retention, as companies can no longer rely solely on high-cost customer acquisition strategies that fail to generate sustainable profits. By creating a comprehensive and engaging brand presence across multiple channels, retailers can not only meet the diverse needs of their customers but also foster long-term relationships that enhance brand loyalty and drive revenue growth.

Another critical factor in all this is ownership of the customer relationship. As a society, we've become far too comfortable with intermediaries and third-party platforms owning access to our customers. But with uncertainty, volatile marketplaces, and changing terms of service, how can we rely on Amazon, Facebook, or anyone else for the success of our business?

For a good reason, first-party data is a strategic goal of many DTC brands. Owning a direct relationship with the customer means using their information intuitively and giving them a highly personalized experience. You can do so much more for them than if you are behind the walls of a well-guarded third-party system like Amazon.

The next era of platforms is already adapting to this truth. Take Shopify, which has seen unprecedented growth with the rise of DTC simply by allowing its platform to be open. Technology companies have created layers of solutions that are all integrated into an ecosystem that enables brands to do incredible business at scale, no matter how small. And they get to keep the customer relationships.

WHAT YOU CAN DO

The technology and strategies exist for any B2B or B2C company to create meaningful and helpful relationships with their customers and to own those relationships. That foundation will weather whatever storm commerce may throw our way. But what often doesn't exist is the mindset.

The most significant step you can make in your business is to embrace the uncertainty, just like a Gen Zer. Uncertainty isn't anything but the stage you're on. Your mission, no matter what is going on in the world, is to be your authentic self. And authentically help the people in your lives and your business world.

DTC is the perfect mindset for this environment because it forces you to think on behalf of the customer and your audience, and the feedback on whether or not it's working is instantaneous. Instead of thinking about how to convince, trick, or compel them to do anything, you must consider how to benefit them. And that approach has served me time and time again. That is indeed the secret to Electriq's success and mine.

Find ways to be helpful; this storm, or whatever may still come, won't get in your way.

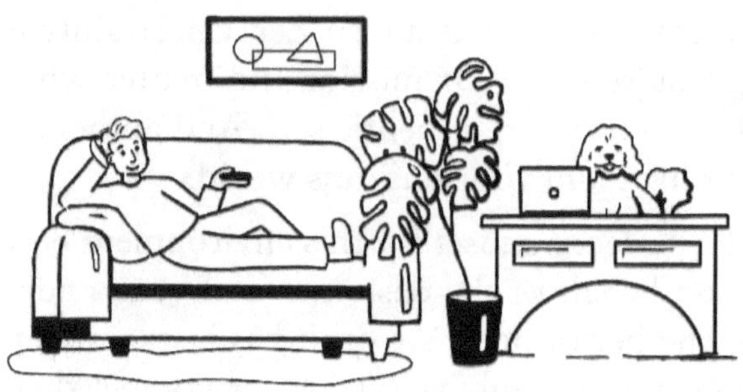

3
DELEGATION IS NOT OPTIONAL

THE IMAGE WE PAINT OF ENTREPRENEURS IS NOT HEALTHY. I think we all have that notion that entrepreneurs work insane hours, have sleepless nights, and never rest. That they put their blood, sweat, and tears into the job, and their entrepreneurial journey takes every minute of every day and every ounce of energy they have. We imagine them sleeping in their offices, never eating, and subsisting on their passion alone.

I think this ideal must be connected in some way to legacy ideals around work ethic. We tend to revere and honor people who work hard, and therefore, hard work becomes a value in and of itself. Whether or not that work produces anything of value is almost beside the point. And entrepreneurs–well, they should work harder than anyone.

This is the life we chose. We are entrepreneurs, and no matter who we are or why we started this journey, we went into it knowing we'd be wearing all the hats.

But it honestly doesn't need to be this way. Building a team around you that complements your strengths and weaknesses is essential to being a successful entrepreneur. So yes, we might wear many hats, especially in the beginning, and it takes long hours, but we should be rigorous about taking those hats off and putting them on other people we trust.

Entering the business world with a Gen Z mindset may fly in the face of generations framing what work should look like. We are seeing this in workplace culture as younger professionals insist on boundaries and favor life in the whole "work/life balance" equation. But this applies to business leaders and entrepreneurs too.

Life is for living. Sure, business is a big part of that–especially for entrepreneurs–but that isn't the only part. And I'd argue that it isn't even the most important part.

Much of what a founder does with this legacy mindset is not what a founder should be doing. The burn-the-midnight-oil entrepreneur is likely managing their business rather than working on it. This fundamental issue is why founders work too hard, burn out too quickly, and cannot build a thriving business.

Here's the reality we all, as entrepreneurs, must face: a founder's job is not management.

It took me far too long to realize this, even though mentors told me and even though I had a fresh business outlook. And it is something that I still struggle with–and I probably always will. But in my journey, I learned some critical principles that helped me escape this trap, even if I fall into it again occasionally. The foundation for these principles is that the founder needs to focus on building and growing the business. If something that does not directly relate to developing and building the company needs to be done, then someone else needs to do it.

THE TRAP

We can't do everything, and we shouldn't try.

I mean, I get it. We're entrepreneurs, and we like to do everything. It's sort of what we're wired to do. We have millions of hats, and we like to wear them all and do so as a badge of honor. And in the beginning, we really do need to do everything. But if we're being honest, even if we don't like doing it, we probably feel like we have to do everything even as the business starts to grow. It is ingrained into our social fabric that the intrepid young business owner must bleed to create their dream. The more we bleed and sweat, the more effective we are.

That approach to entrepreneurship is from another era.

It doesn't work now, and I would argue it never did. It's an unnecessary self-sacrificial point of view that is tied into ideals far older than we are and working on assumptions that are simply false.

I fell into this trap hard.

The first real challenge I encountered when building my business was the elusive "back office." Going into this, I didn't think it was a big deal. It was just a matter of keeping up on QuickBooks, processing invoices, handling receivables, and paying taxes. It just didn't feel like much of a burden at any one moment.

But that's a red flag. That's the trap.

The entrepreneur is thinking to themselves, "Oh, it's no big deal, it doesn't take me a lot of time," forgetting that every little thing adds up. And after a while, all of these little tasks pile up until their ship sinks from a thousand leaks.

If I had it to do over again, I would have detailed my process and given it to a different team member far sooner. Looking back, it seems so wrong to me. The CEO of a thriving and growing business should refrain from handling back-office work. They should be building their business.

My mentors told me this, and I suppose I didn't think their delegation advice applied to smaller tasks or a bootstrapped, cash-conscious small business. Often, I fell into the trap of, "I'm too busy to train someone else to do this properly, so I am just going to keep doing it myself." It might take 3 hours to offload a 1-hour per week task, but it's important to find those 3 hours to save those 1-hours from adding up. But I kept it on my plate too long. There are countless tasks like that, and those deliverables could be sourced by someone else who would do it better.

That struggle doesn't go away. I'm still dealing with it.

THE OTHER TRAP

I'm just going to say it. Micromanagement.

I get it. I do. We are business leaders, which is highly personal, especially if we started the business. So we want things to go a certain way. We want things to be successful. And so we have difficulty letting go.

We may have built roles and filled them with good people, but we don't trust them to do what they were hired to do. We manage them every step of the way. And it might not even be because we don't think they'll do a good job. It's just that we are afraid they'll miss a step, do it differently enough that there will be problems, or that they couldn't possibly know all of the nuances of the business and make the most optimal decisions.

One of the most challenging things I had to do as I delegated more responsibilities was wrapping my mind around being okay with 9/10 execution instead of 10/10. In an ideal world, everything you delegate would be to someone who can do it BETTER than you. However, the reality is that you will be the subject matter expert for some things, but it still makes sense for you to delegate, given there are higher priority items for you.

And when we build teams with people who have to get our approval on every step they make or are accustomed to us checking in on their work too frequently, we cultivate a culture of dependence.

We are building a business that requires us to be involved at every level. And our team members don't feel as bought into the business because they're not truly building it with you; they're simply executing tasks for you. This also makes your business significantly less valuable in an acquisition.

In these situations, we are becoming a bottleneck for the organization and can literally choke it to the point where it cannot grow—or worse, begins to whither.

Inserting yourself into too many aspects of the business and directly managing the people you've brought on board means that you will focus much more on day-to-day deliverables than business growth. And who will be if you are not focused on business growth and where the company should be heading?

Managers manage, and founders build.

If a founder is managing, the organization must move at the whim of that one person. And there is only one person. So how can an organization grow or be flexible if a single person with a finite amount of dwindling time daily binds it?

There are also things that we really have no business doing. Certain activities are outside our wheelhouse, and we can get into trouble if we do them wrong.

I should have set up a payroll provider from day one, even if it felt too expensive. It would have saved me a lot of headaches. I used a consultant to process it manually with the various states, which was a nightmare, especially when hiring remotely. Now with a fully remote office, it's essential.

You have different rules and requirements for each state, county, and local laws and regulations that need to be applied, fees, and registration processes. This was challenging until I onboarded a payroll provider who handled all that. The payroll provider also provides healthcare insurance, a substantial benefit for any company when hiring talent.

I FOUND ALL THIS OUT THE HARD WAY

In the beginning, I was a freelancer. I put on all of the hats and moved from project to project. The moment I shifted into an agency structure, everything changed. The primary difference between the two models is that in freelancing, I was only responsible for my work, which is a thousand times easier than being accountable for the work of even one other individual. The difference was dramatic when it came to client satisfaction and ensuring that there was a level of quality control on the work product.

Even though it was a one-person shop, I always positioned my freelancing as an agency. I was really not an agency. All it took to change that was hiring my first employee.

That was the tipping point. Now other people are working on clients here. I was still responsible for my own work product, but I was also responsible for another team member. And that has only increased as we've grown.

Now it only felt like Electriq was something beyond just a lifestyle business once we started to get into that 11-12 employee range. And especially when we started onboarding new clients whom I was no longer involved in the sales process and had never even spoken to. That was the biggest jump for me. We now had clients I had zero interaction with. I did not sell them, and I wouldn't be working with them either. The Electriq team was now empowered to do that.

One of the things I learned early on is how important confidence is in client management and retention. There was no one directing me on what to do. There was no one watching my workflow or guiding my strategy. So I needed to be confident that I knew what I was doing and that I could be a strategic thinker and creatively solve problems.

Why? When companies decide to work with an agency, they are looking for subject matter expertise and strategy first and foremost. They aren't hiring you to work with a robot who just says yes to whatever directive is given.

They want a strategic thinker who brings new ideas and pushes back on things when they don't think it's correct.

One of the most important things I did when delegating sales and working with clients was engraining this philosophy and mindset around confidence among the entire team. If I had the confidence in them to do this, they should have confidence in themselves.

> *A Personal Story: We had, and still have, a very talented and capable team member who started working with Electriq right out of college. He was a quick learner and knew his stuff, but he needed improvement with client communications. At first, I couldn't possibly understand why. He was one of our most talented team members. But after joining a client call, I immediately understood the issue. When presenting strategy or ideas, it was almost being phrased as a question, as if he was looking to the client for validation that what he was saying was, in fact, true. Now, I knew what he was saying made a ton of sense and would work, but the client didn't feel secure or that they were working with an expert because it wasn't projected confidently. After working with him, he's one of our strongest client-facing team members. It had nothing to do with knowledge. It had everything to do with confidence. It's on YOU as the founder to instill that confidence in your team.*

SELF-MOTIVATION

The other important thing I learned, especially during the early stages, is the ability to motivate yourself and manage your schedule and time extremely efficiently. No boss is telling you what to do. No one is giving you meetings, schedules, or work plans. Your time and effort into your business is entirely up to you.

And you need to find a happy medium and balance. Working 120 hours a week for the rest of your life is unrealistic. Sure, there might be some weeks where you do, but it's finding what's sustainable for you and what will allow you to thrive.

That inevitably led to me needing to delegate.

The best way to do this is to write down everything I did (I spent a solid week doing this). I wrote down everything—whether it was a one-off random item, a meeting, handling payroll, or handling client work. Whatever it was. I listed everything.

I was shocked about how many random tasks on that list were better suited to someone who is an expert in that role. Should I really be doing bookkeeping?

After that week, I split each task into two categories. The first category included all of the items I should still be doing. The second category includes everything else that needs to be delegated elsewhere. Then, I started dividing out which tasks could be handled by someone internal on the team or required a new hire to come on board.

Even after all of this, I still had yet to delegate everything. For example, I still sent month-end client billing to ensure it was done 100% correctly, and I used it to review our month-end P&L. It only took about an hour or so every month. But still. This stuff adds up. That is the perfect example of something I should have handed off to someone sooner rather than later.

That's twelve hours a year.

I could use that time to build processes for scale and focus on the strategic long-term direction of Electriq.

It is critical to know where and how you can provide the most value to your company as it continues to grow.

MISTAKES WERE MADE

There is a flip side to the delegation coin.

Assuming you did what I did and ruthlessly culled your daily activities by offloading tasks to your team, you may find yourself in a situation where the person you entrusted these tasks to didn't take those tasks as seriously as you would have.

I made that mistake. I identified the proper role for the tasks, but someone other than the right person to fill that role. So I quickly promoted them internally into a position like management before they were ready for that position. Once in place, I offloaded my tasks onto their desks and became very confused when things didn't work out as expected.

In retrospect, I should have asked. People will tell you if they don't believe they are ready. And you can talk with them about what they need to get to that point so you can lift them up and help them get there. People will be honest if you open the conversation up and sometimes they'd prefer you hire externally rather than put them in a position where they know they can't be successful.

> *One of the most important things I learned during my time building Electriq is that NOT everyone wants to be a manager.*

Certain people work very well with ambiguity and the freedom to build their processes and ways. But others prefer structure and guidance. I avoid making assumptions that everyone is like me. Team members are individuals with different wants and needs.

Good to know and good to remember!

THE DELEGATION SWEET SPOT

In the beginning, the delegation process was entirely about getting things off my desk and onto another person's–whether that was because they were better than me at it or because it wasn't something I should be spending my mental bandwidth doing. However, delegation was happening much more on a macro level as things progressed. Team members and managers are delegating to other people.

That's important. Because I want managers and team members focused on where they should be focused. So I help them figure out how to delegate and elevate people within their departments.

There may be cases where we delegate outside the organization altogether. That could be for back-end and accounting, but it could also be for expertise outside of our company services or simply someone outside the organization helping us improve.

There is a wide range of activities that I now systemically delegate, giving me the space I need to have to focus on company growth.

Team members help with my calendar and coordinating schedules. They interface with clients and put together reporting decks (something I used to do monthly–30 client reporting decks! Every month!). I've delegated our signature agency audit process. I would do very work-intensive processes like web, email, SMS, lifecycle retention, social, SEO, content—basically everything. I rarely touch any of it now.

Now, I have professionals on my team that do that for Electriq (and better than me). Team members organize the audit, and a specialist from each department focuses on their field, providing specialized feedback that I would never have been capable of providing before.

We can't be experts in everything. That's what teams are for.

DELEGATION IS ABOUT MORE THAN WORKFLOW

It's really about focus. Where are you focused? Where is your team focused? This also means taking a look at where your business is focused. Because if the company focuses on too many things, no amount of delegation will save you.

A focused business means saying no to prospective clients or businesses that do not align with and just don't make sense for your company's long-term goal and vision.

We took on a couple of B2B clients and non-Shopify clients because revenue was revenue. That revenue could immediately go back into hiring new team members allowing us to scale.

But some of those relationships never should have been entered into, to begin with. Not that they went bad, but even if they didn't go south, you're still distracting your team from your core competencies and focus.

We still have some B2B clients today with whom we do great work. We have a strong relationship with them, but I think we'd be better off if we only did e-commerce. So we don't take on any new B2B clients now because it has become a distraction from our core services.

We can't and shouldn't be everything to everyone. Otherwise, we're not going to be good at anything.

> *We are a retention marketing agency for Shopify Plus brands trying to increase the LTV of their customers.*

Being good at a clearly defined thing is vital for various reasons. First, you can deliver on a promise in a way that a jack-of-all-trades competitor can't. You become specialists, and by being specialists, your services become more valuable. Will you pay more for a general practitioner or a brain surgeon when you have to have brain surgery? Well, maybe that's an extreme example, but you get the point.

Additionally, many start-ups have an eye toward getting acquired. To become valuable to potential buyers, going all in on a couple of critical areas is far more effective. Those acquiring businesses usually look to fill a gap in their business, so they aren't looking for a jack-of-all-trades.

In the case of the agency, for example, because we're so heavy into Shopify, the tech stack ecosystem, email/SMS marketing, and development, it's significantly easier for another agency or software company to see how we can plug into their current business and make our combination greater than the sum of our partners. In our case, we did get acquired by a software company specifically looking for Shopify expertise and the ability to help educate an entire industry on best practices for Shopify.

If we were a BigCommerce Shopify WooCommerce, SEO, content, email, Web, this and that all over the place, super spread out, not really focused agency, we wouldn't have as much value to a potential business trying to acquire you because it's harder to integrate. And there's not as much synergy there, nor is there as much potential opportunity.

> *A Note about Specialization: We did not specialize right away, and that was important for us. How else would I know what we truly were best at if we didn't tip our toes into everything?*

DELEGATION LEADS TO EXPERTS

When delegating to the team, I gave them the power and authority to handle my assigned tasks or projects. Over time, they became experts in that category so I could elevate their position and give them even more autonomy. By doing this, I didn't need to worry about a traditional resume or number of years of experience when hiring; I knew I could just find someone willing to own their work.

I found value in pushing for and allowing internal growth instead of trying to hire from the outside on top of the existing team. And as it relates to onboarding and training team members, I documented our internal processes and procedures. That effort was ramped up to include professional development content for new team members so they had access to continuing education from a wealth of knowledge within the agency. It also helped them get up to speed with the latest tools and technologies to do their jobs better.

Planning for growth this way must happen at the very start, even before you start employing people.

By giving control to your trusted team, you can create a culture of experts, ultimately creating a more effective and valuable company.

Letting go of work is good for business!

DIFFERENT MINDSET

I was in the workforce long enough to see that this approach is not standard.

Delegation in other companies meant that a middle manager would assign a task, tell you precisely what to do with it, and harp on you until it was done.

Micromanagement is not delegation—or at least not an effective way to delegate.

The mindset in legacy companies is more about telling someone what to do and ensuring they do it right. This creates a "gotcha" culture, a lot of unnecessary management time, and can lead to toxic work cultures.

The revolt we see with Gen Z in the workplace has much to do with that mindset. They are not trusted to do what they were assigned and must defend their work at every turn. It leads them to check out or "quiet quit."

At the same time, autonomy can also be abused if there isn't accountability. Make sure you set specific KPIs and OKRs up so your team is evaluated against something. Otherwise, you might find yourself with a team member working another full-time job outside of your organization with all that freedom you gave them!

I've found a trusting form of delegation, which empowers teams to have the authority to do the job in their way, is far more effective. It is built on a culture of trust and requires a lot of faith from the business leader. And while there is a risk that the work will not be done right or the team will fail, you've allowed them to learn from those mistakes.

Healthy delegation yields healthy teams, and healthy teams yield healthy organizations.

THINGS ARE MORE COMPLICATED

The idea of delegation is becoming far more critical now that there is a work from home movement due to the pandemic. We were forced to create processes and mechanisms to manage workflow across remote teams and have since settled into a new way of doing things.

I have mixed feelings about WFH. I really like a lot about it, and it has allowed me to expand the team in unexpected ways. It will enable people to move wherever they desire. We've even seen quite a shift in the housing market of where people are headed now that they aren't stuck in certain cities based on a job position.

In the future, a hybrid approach to work will make the most sense. There are significant pros to having an in-person workspace where team members can come in and have that human interaction and get the ability to collaborate. But there are a lot of pros to being able to work from anywhere and having that freedom and autonomy to get up and move and travel the world while still handling your duties. And so, there will be a happy medium, and one way is not necessarily right or wrong.

That being said, I would never start a new company remote-first. Those first months/years and having the founding team together for collaboration are crucial to setting up a foundation for success.

Some companies may stay fully remote, and then others will have to return to 9-5 based on their industry. But for me, I plan on making a hybrid approach where there's an office, and maybe once a week, everyone is required to come in for in-person meetings, but otherwise, team members are free to choose what works best for them. Employees should WANT to come into the office at the end of the day.

Everyone's preference for how and where they get work done is different. It's essential to keep this in mind when structuring your workspace requirements.

If this is the new normal, then micro-management and older mindsets about delegation are not feasible. Companies are finding it impossible to trace all of their employees' work. When the work is done satisfactorily (albeit unconventional), it becomes clear that micro-management is pointless and costly.

There will always be businesses where WFH flexibility will be a challenge. But this is the new normal; the sooner we shift our mindset to accommodate it, the better.

Teams are not asking for much. They just want to be trusted and respected. They want boundaries and flexibility. Our job as business leaders is to build the systems they need to succeed and support them as they manage their work.

I view delegation as a form of support or a framework for building processes so teams can be independent and successful. And that mindset is the major shift from older views on business. It is also the mindset that will make businesses more effective and resilient during uncertainty.

4
ITERATION IS LIFE

ONE OF THE SECRETS TO MY SUCCESS IS THAT I basically had no idea what I was doing, and I still embrace that mentality and try to learn as much as I can wherever I can.

I started as a freelancer to put my skills to good use and just make some spending money in college. When I started seeing results, I took up any work I thought could grow my business. Maybe I needed a testimonial—perhaps I just needed cash. There was no real strategy behind my business development except to grow, grow, grow. I fell into the Shopify ecosystem early because I saw tremendous potential—particularly for small businesses needing to find an accessible product channel and connect directly with their customers.

But that wasn't even my focus, even though it became the core of my business and the catalyst that led to an acquisition.

When my practice fell into a rhythm shortly after college, I was primarily focused on SEO and content. Then we got to the point where we expanded social media, refined our craft, and started positioning ourselves around the fact we were a Gen Z business with a new approach to things. Then came email and SMS, website design, and development. Ultimately, we specialized in customer experience and retention marketing, shedding the services that weren't in our sweet spot, resulting in a hockey stick of growth for us. Our sales and messaging strategy was cleaner and more effective, while our team was able to produce better results.

I didn't know what I didn't know, and I don't think I had one penultimate goal that I was constantly striving for. Except for growth. How do we continue to get bigger? How do we continue to get more clients? How do we continue to make more revenue? I was super focused on growth as a goal because I needed it to sustain itself long-term, and the growth excited me. So while there was no master plan, there was an approach. I wanted to avoid getting bogged down in a single vision or way of doing things. I needed to constantly adapt, improve things, refine the process and vision, and double down on what we were good at. We needed to be adaptable and quick to pivot.

Above all of that, I saw Shopify was where the potential was. And where my joy was. The idea of creating stores, aggregating zero-party data, mapping customer journeys, architecting Shopify tech stacks–that was the exciting stuff. And all of the prior expertise started coming together.

Now we're a lifecycle marketing, customer experience and retention agency with an alcohol technology parent company focused on bringing alcohol online. We still do SEO and social and work with non-wine accounts, but they are all engineered to support what's truly important–lifetime value. The point is it's an evolution.

Businesses thrive on iteration. If we did not iterate based on the needs in the market or the business opportunities that present themselves, we would have remained stagnant as an SEO and social company with no differentiation amidst an armada of other SEO and social companies, and we certainly wouldn't have been acquired for a larger purpose.

Common wisdom tells businesses to specialize and focus. That is true–especially with the need to differentiate in today's cluttered and uncertain world. But that doesn't mean stopping. That doesn't mean stagnating. And that certainly doesn't mean you don't ever change.

THE TWO BROKEN ORGANIZATIONAL FOUNDATIONS

Let's tackle the legacy mindset here. If we accept that the world is in a permanent state of uncertainty, the foundations of legacy businesses may not hold well—even if they have existed for a long time.

This book will probably be useless in five years, except for the underlying framework.

The way I see it, the legacy mindset yields one of two business foundations that, while they may have worked in more certain times, are now buckling under the weight of our new era. The first is Everything to Everyone. I'd argue this was a fallacy even in the best of times. But the idea here is that brands generalize in their field and try accommodating every potential customer and business need.

In the agency world, we call these businesses "generalists." They are the ones that raise their hand for every service request whether or not they have experience in that field, because they can figure it out.

It is a people-pleaser modus operandi that often stretches businesses too thin as they try to scramble from project to project, yielding moderate to inadequate results.

This was Electriq in the early days as I grasped for revenue at every turn and ignored every piece of advice I ever received or business book I read! But, we were early on, and I was still trying to figure out what we are best at and, more importantly, what energizes us. Once I found it, I knew it was time to specialize and go all in.

The second broken foundation is the Rock of Ages. These businesses may specialize and have a well-tuned practice, but they are immobile, inflexible, and unmoving. While that makes for a sturdy business, they buckle if enough pressure is applied. Immovable companies cannot be resilient because they don't have the flexibility to handle changing tides.

While Electriq is a specialized agency, that doesn't mean we're not looking for opportunities. In 2023, we're adding direct mail and push notification capabilities to our marketing arm and a community management division, supporting our ability to improve our #1 goal - increase CLTV.

Again in specific business environments, both Everything to Everyone and Rock of Ages could thrive. The E2E folks could people-please and burn through resources as much as they want. And even though their services weren't great and they'd lose customers, it was cheap enough and easy enough to get new ones. The RoA folks could just withstand by being who they were. No one else could do the specific thing they could do so well, so they wouldn't need to worry about competition. And any changing tide would not affect them because someone always needed their specialty.

Well, things have changed. The tide is unpredictable. The very ground we stand on is unpredictable. We cannot forecast five years, let alone one or two. We don't know how the marketplace will shift, what technologies will be available, and what global populations will demand. All we know for sure is that we don't know anything.

So how can an E2E organization afford the resources needed to keep up with the constantly changing demands of their market if they are willing to do everything that crosses their path? How can an RoA organization quickly adapt if they are so rooted in their specialty it would take systemic changes to keep up with new services?

THAT'S WHY BUSINESS LEADERS ARE PANICKING

We see it all around us. There is a huge backlash against the WFH movement, a free fall in response to the higher customer acquisition costs, and a widespread lack of confidence from investors. Everything from workplace culture to marketing and communications strategies is in flux.

Companies with the legacy mindset are shutting off spending, laying off staff by the shipload, cleaving entire departments, and casting blame on inflation, economic instability, and other macro trends.

Business leaders are discovering that their way of doing things is no longer working. Even though it has worked for them for years, and with the world rapidly changing around them, they may not know the best way forward. Strategy is out the window, and tactics are thrown against the wall hoping that something will work.

But then some companies are thriving. They can adapt and withstand any shift or change from macro trends. While they are still on shaky ground, they have built a strong company culture and foundation for times like these.

Those are the companies that have different mindsets focused on resiliency and flexibility.

Those are the companies that practice value iteration.

MY INITIAL EVERYTHING TO EVERYONE PROBLEM

When I started the agency, we provided a laundry list of services we don't do now, even two years later. If you had even come to me a year and a half ago and asked what we do, I would have told you completely different things.

My business journey was rooted in learning. I learned a lot about people and leadership. And I learned about what doesn't work. Since I had no agency background, I built things the way I thought they should be, with no frame of reference on traditional structures. That forced me to be aware of whether or not my approach worked. Sure, there were some things I would've been able to start with from the get-go that would've been valuable. Still, there are also many things I didn't do from the get-go that led to other ideas, best practices, and organizational structures that were a differentiation for us.

My not knowing what I was doing was a hurdle compared to seasoned agency professionals who start independently regarding their network, access to new clients, credibility, etc. But, the positive side was that nothing I was doing was concrete. I was super aware of the process and watched closely if things worked. Had I been entrenched in a "way of doing things," I wouldn't have noticed the failures so quickly and easily.

I checked my work relentlessly. The primary way of doing this was by creating and cultivating a feedback loop with clients and team members. I cultivated a role for Client Success Managers and defined agency processes, and then we made our solutions scalable after we found what worked.

It's still not perfect. We are constantly iterating to make it better for ourselves and our clients.

Iteration was key and continues to be so. I do not want to be stuck in old ways or old thoughts.

That's truly what allows us to shine and thrive. I don't think that you can or should get locked into long-term plans–at least, I prefer not to get tuned to those minutiae. I think about direction–where we are heading and where we want to go. But I'm not locked into an immovable goal or vision. I love to take an approach to crafting an overarching strategy that entails three key components:

1. How do you want to be viewed in a year, and where do you want to be?

2. What are the strategies you'll use to get there?

3. What are the tactics you'll deploy against your strategies?

That thinking leads me to a strategy or multiple strategies. From there, I can refine tactics–the daily things I need to do to get the agency toward the strategy, leading to the end goal.

THE DIFFERENCE BETWEEN STRATEGY AND TACTICS

Strategy is a long-term plan to achieve a goal; it determines what needs to be done and why. Tactics are short-term actions taken to achieve that goal. Strategy is more challenging to change once it's set in motion, whereas tactics are easier to adjust.

Strategies define tactics and not the other way around.

Let's use Electriq as an example. This is the exact exercise I went through at the end of 2020.

1. Where I wanted us to be in a year: The #1 Shopify Plus Retention Marketing Agency

2. Strategies

    a. Changing Agency Perception

    b. Increase Revenue

    c. Become a Thought Leader in Ecommerce

3. Tactics to Support These Strategies

    a. Create an agency 1-pager, build landing pages around our specific expertise, and update all messaging to be around our Retention-as-a-Service offering (RaaS).

    b. Invest in team member training, revamp client-facing materials, achieve top-tier tech partner certifications, and update our contracts.

    c. Publish a weekly newsletter, launch a podcast, create white papers, and speak at conferences.

Too often, businesses go straight into tactics and get lost in the day-to-day while losing sight of where they want to be heading and what sort of strategies they need to develop to achieve their goal.

WHERE TO FOCUS

I was so steadfast in growing and scaling the business that we said yes to things that honestly made zero sense for us to say yes to. And for a while, we used to service B2B and e-commerce brands and clients because I couldn't say no to additional revenue, no matter how small.

That hampered us early on because I knew that additional revenue gave me more resources to hire more team members to service more clients.

It was a flywheel. We just kept spinning and spinning. Before long, our team stretched too thin and consistently worked in areas needing more expertise. And we had clients that could have been a better fit.

If there's anything I could have done differently, it is understanding that turning away business does not necessarily mean we aren't going to scale as quickly. If we had said no to specific businesses, we would have been stronger with some of our clients, which made more sense. We also would have been better positioned to capitalize on the new opportunities that were the right fit.

And so maybe one month you aren't just crushing new sales because the prospects that came in the door weren't the right fit.

That's okay.

Understanding that you don't have to make everyone work within your system is powerful because if you only invest in the brands you think will be successful with your agency, you're just setting yourself up for long-term success. You'll have lower client churn–a critical metric when we need to focus on retention as a strategy over the immense cost of finding and onboarding new clients.

Just the other day, we turned away a $150,000 development project because it was outside our wheelhouse. It's still painful for me to see that. But I've gotten to the point where I'm comfortable with it because I know we need to focus on what we're good at.

IT'S A BALANCE

The challenge here is balancing a niche focus but not getting so stuck in that focus that you can't maneuver and iterate. Suppose you can figure out how to find the right balance between focusing on your specialized niche and staying adaptable. In that case, you'll have the resilience to grow, even if your world is constantly in flux.

I've found a good strategy for striking this balance is to focus on specific areas of the business where you have existing expertise but keep the doors open for that expertise to grow and change. For example, our agency was very good at retention strategies, particularly with email and SMS, so we shifted focus to that.

But then, as we strengthened our position within the Shopify ecosystem, we were able to iterate and fine-tune our offering to be focused on retention services for Shopify only. Then, it was further narrowed down to retention marketing for Shopify Plus brands on Klaviyo and Attentive.

So we were able to continually narrow our focus while at the same time keeping our strategy flexible enough to iterate. Sometimes many times per year. It also means we can capitalize on our goals much easier because we don't need to shift our entire organization to meet changing needs. We can simply iterate.

Our vision stays constant, but our strategies and tactics evolve.

We also need to be open to changing course. Suppose we were entirely locked in on a particular approach to digital marketing, for example, and not open to changing the strategy based on changing circumstances in the marketplace. In that case, we'd still be crunching high-labor SEO work, which wouldn't have been a valuable acquisition for a potential buyer. Just because we can do something doesn't mean it is the only thing we should do. Nor does it mean that is all we should ever do. Too many companies get stuck in their niche and do not even entertain the option of shifting course or strategy. Specialization and niching are good, but getting stuck is not.

Businesses are organisms. They need to have room and air to breathe so they can grow. They need to be nimble and respond to a changing environment. They need to evolve and improve.

Iteration as a business strategy is an important posture for our times. And the willingness to do so and to adapt and fine-tune the business model frequently makes companies resilient. And it is different from how I see businesses being run.

THIS ISN'T JUST ABOUT BEING NIMBLE

"Lean" and "nimble" are not new to business strategy conversations. I understand that flexibility has always been sound business. But I think it's important to reiterate that this is not just in the abstract. It's not just a suggestion. It is essential to exist peacefully in this new era. It is table stakes to having a thriving business and a thriving life.

Economic disruptions happen whenever there is a global shock. And as the *Harvard Business Review* points out these "global shocks" are happening more and more frequently. And now it's basically at the point where disruption is the new normal.

We are seeing uncertainty in the sociopolitical world where politics have become highly toxic and divisive, in the energy world as we all scramble for resources, the pandemic continues without any end in sight, war–the list goes on. But on the technology sid, things are just as uncertain. One day the world's biggest social media platform connects businesses to consumers. The next, it's the Old West. One day an entire generation will embrace Instagram. Next, they are on TikTok. Artificial Intelligence is completely changing everything about everything.

How can a business plan for that? How can it plan for anything?

I'm not suggesting we don't come up with plans. But I recommend the plan should include the idea that we don't know what will happen.

That's where resiliency comes in. That's why iteration is key. That's why my business is focused on retaining customers rather than getting new ones. We must understand that we can only control ourselves and our ability to adapt.

5

TEAM MEMBERS ARE PARTNERS

A quick note before beginning this chapter. While your team members are your partners, you can NEVER expect your team members to work as long or as "hard" as you do. It's unfair, unreasonable, and unrealistic. At the end of the day, you are the owner of the business. Would you work as hard for someone else's company as you do for your own?

FIND PEOPLE THAT ARE BETTER THAN YOU ARE AT WHAT they do and let them own their work from top to bottom. The biggest difference between a legacy business mindset and a Gen Z one is that older models view people as resources. Well, they certainly are! But the idea that they are a "resource" in the same way a computer or software platform is–that's the problem. The view of people and teams in a more resilient mindset embraces the human element more.

People are resources, and they are assets. But they are not numbers, and they are not things. They have goals, emotions, context, background, and home lives. They are beautifully infallible, creative, textured, layered, and complex. They have opinions, hopes, ideas, points of view, and life experiences. Yes, businesses employ them to do a service, but they also invest themselves in that business. Understanding the nuance makes a company more resilient–especially in times when keeping people seems to be a hard thing to do. If this sounds obvious to you, it is. But I've seen countless businesses get lost in scaling and lose sight of their team's humanity.

Companies must treat their employees as partners, not assets, to get the best out of their employees. That means valuing their input and ideas and giving them a voice in the company. It also means being willing to invest in their training and development and listening to them when they have concerns or suggestions.

Employees who are valued partners in the company will be more productive and committed to their work. They will also be more loyal, meaning they're less likely to jump ship when a different opportunity comes. Treating employees as partners is not just the right thing to do – it's good for business.

You're not hiring right if you don't view your team members as partners. Anecdotes from the ecosystem about our team continue to reinforce how valuable we are collectively,

We're going to unpack why empowering employees is a sound business strategy, not just a nice thing to do.

PEOPLE FIRST?

Every company says they want to be a people-first company, but when push comes to shove, they really aren't.

To the many workers who contributed to the Great Resignation, it's no secret why it happened. Countless TikTok monologues told us the primary reason was they did not feel like their role mattered or that the value they brought to the role was appreciated. Employees were treated as assets instead of partners, and they eventually left. The Great Resignation was a wake-up call for businesses everywhere, and some are slowly starting to realize that if they want to keep their employees, they need to start treating them like people.

Companies have treated their teams like commodities since the dawn of the working class, valuing their output over their input. They have been focusing on the bottom line instead of the people who actually contribute to it. As a result, when the pandemic revealed to everyone that life was short, they started walking out in droves.

Employees must feel valued and listened to by their employers if the company expects them to stay long-term. And businesses need to be willing to invest in their employees if they want them to be productive and successful.

I've heard all sides during the pandemic about the workforce. I've heard that employers don't respect their teams, that micro-management is toxic, and that teams are expected to compromise their well-being for the company's sake. I've also heard from the other side that people don't want to work anymore, are just phoning it in, and don't care, and that one's value to an organization is earned.

And look, I get it. I'm an employer. I can relate to the frustrations of founders and managers about how without accountability, teams may not deliver to your expectations. But the fact is, as a society, we've overcorrected on that. Some people won't deliver if they are not micro-managed or held accountable. But that doesn't make it the proper leadership position for everyone. We assume the masses are lazy opportunists rather than understanding edge cases for what they are – edge cases.

Do you really want to hire someone you need to micromanage? That was my #1 criterion for hiring at Electriq. You needed to be a self-starter who we could count on.

The Great Resignation and Quiet Quitting are the symptoms of a much larger problem. People are putting up boundaries, and companies are recoiling in indignation. This is happening because people have had enough. They don't want to be a commodity. They want to be valued, and they want to have a high quality of life. Yes, even working life.

And I've realized as I started building teams, I've learned that respecting people's boundaries, giving them the power to own their jobs, making sure they are heard, and giving them the freedom to have a thriving personal life is good business.

Thriving people make a thriving business.

MY FIRST HIRE

I'm shocked that the first team member I hired at Electriq didn't quit within the first day she came into our office–and I will put in air quotes. It was a small (now defunct) little co-working space in Chinatown, Los Angeles, tucked away in an area that is not necessarily the nicest or most riveting area to work.

We had an office that could fit four people buried in the back corner with no natural light or anything a human needs to survive. It was a dungeon. I liked it because I just went into my cave and worked twelve hours a day. But the fact that my first team member didn't run away at first sight of it is shocking.

My furry four-legged partner Bella was a great ice breaker when I conducted my first actual job interview. It was the first time I was on the other side. I kept it casual and laid back and didn't want it to feel stuffy or very corporate–which would have been laughable if I tried to even do that because of the situation we are in at that point.

And once she finally accepted the position, we moved forward in what I suppose was onboarding. I would be lying if I said there was any onboarding process whatsoever. It involved two steps: arriving at the office and getting to work. So I put her in a position to help me start to build out processes and create what Electriq would become.

There was some light training, and I delivered an ad hoc data dump about everything I had been doing. But I still needed to fully understand how important it was to document all of my processes and make sure that we were set up to scale efficiently where I wasn't doing everything one to one.

After that, our hiring process was very informal, and decisions all came down to the reality that we had new clients coming into the door that we couldn't service with existing resources. We needed to go bigger. And so that's how it was for a while. Since we were bootstrapped and I didn't have any money, we would hire just in time or a little bit retroactively, and I would have to fill in the gaps as those new team members got up to speed.

But once we got to a specific size, we could hire looking towards the future and bring somebody on for two weeks, three weeks, even a month, maybe longer, where they aren't actively servicing clients. Instead, they're completing all of our onboarding and training procedures, internal projects and getting up to speed with how we work with clients. While we're at that point now, early on, it was reactive, not proactive. But I put myself in the new team members' shoes and asked what I would need or want to feel set up for success at a company if it wasn't mine.

So I didn't give a lot of thought to cultivating culture.

Even at our size now, I still meet with every team member 1:1 when they start. For starters, I think it's important for the whole team to know an organization's leader and allow each team member to ask questions and learn. In these meetings, I always stress 2 things: 1) If there is anything you do not agree with or think we could be doing better, vocalize it!!! Whether it's the onboarding process, our client communications, or how we report, it doesn't matter. Everyone at Electriq is expected to bring valuable ideas, not just execute on a roadmap; and 2) I am just a Slack away if you ever need ANYTHING.

But doing what I was doing started creating the culture of the business. I've only wanted to provide my team with all the freedom they need to succeed. In the beginning, I went too far with that; some team members weren't ready for that level of autonomy and ownership. But others thrived on it, took up the challenge, and have grown. They are still with me today.

WHEN I BUILT MY TEAMS

Things went smoothly for me in the beginning. But that's because I didn't know what I was doing. Looking back, I was hamstrung by the complexities of business and just thought I was supposed to be the one to manage all of that. It was annoying then, but I didn't realize the value of building a team that handled these things.

Everything from taxes to registering with local state authorities when I started hiring employees out of state. It even becomes more complex with the various legal rules and requirements, the accounting, the accounts receivables–all that non-glamorous stuff that nobody really tells you about when you start off on your entrepreneurial journey and things you have to do yourself in the beginning.

Now I'd rather be focused on growing the business and doing what I do best. Back office and management are necessary, but it isn't my role.

That was the first lesson I learned. Bring in experts to handle the stuff you're bad at so you can focus on the stuff you're good at.

But most importantly, trust them to do it enough that you can let go.

We learned so much about the hiring process. In the beginning, we'd just interview everyone. There was so much wasted time. And there was a lot of noise on LinkedIn where people would randomly apply, even when we didn't have positions for them.

Amidst the flow of resumes, countless interviews, and interactions on social media, a particular approach began to emerge. It became clear that applicants were cut from a specific cloth and were prepared to move into a structured corporate environment or came from institutional marketing environments. My approach started focusing on those that were outside of the rhythm of that.

Even as early as high school, when I was working internships, I felt the thing that needed to change the most in the business world was autonomy and ownership of team members. Too much emphasis is put on experience. Even entry-level positions are calling for applicants to have so much experience under their belt they would have had to work for free for years.

The internships I experienced were hierarchical in that you only focused on a defined role for two or three years. Either you moved on, or you didn't. That hierarchy, instruction, and organization are acceptable for some organizations but unnecessarily drive a "level-up" progression in a career defined by time. It shouldn't be. Careers should be forged by how much one is willing to invest and how good one is in their position.

Experience matters, but it's not the end-all-be-all. Sure, in some industries, it matters more than most, but in tech and ecommerce, I want the young, hungry, entrepreneurially-minded spirit of someone who wants to learn and grow.

I constantly found myself waiting in line for my turn at better positions, not because I wasn't invested or effective, but because I was younger. I often found I wasn't listened to, even about matters for which I had a strong opinion, because I hadn't yet earned my stripes.

I knew early on that I didn't want that. I want everyone to have a voice–whether you've been with the company for a day or five years and whether you've just graduated or been in the marketing world for 20 years.

All that it comes down to is who does a great job, and who's invested in the company, who wants to take the initiative and ownership and bring things to life. And that's how my approach cultivated a team with a unique culture.

QUARTERLY FEEDBACK LOOPS

As an entrepreneur, one of the most effective strategies I implemented at Electriq was a structured, quarterly feedback loop that engaged every team member in the company's decision-making process. This approach fostered a sense of ownership among employees and helped identify areas for improvement and innovation that might otherwise have been overlooked.

At the beginning of each quarter, I invited every team member to submit three suggestions for things they believed Electriq should be doing but still needed to address. These ideas range from operational improvements to new product offerings or even changes in company culture. Once all the suggestions were collected, I compiled them into a comprehensive presentation deck.

During a 60-90 minute all-hands meeting, I reviewed each suggestion with the entire team. For each item, I explained how we were addressing it, how we planned to address it in the future, how we might be addressing it in an alternative manner, or why we couldn't prioritize it then. This open discussion provided valuable insights into the team's collective wisdom and ensured everyone's ideas were considered and acknowledged.

The feedback loop proved to be invaluable for Electriq's growth and success. By giving team members a voice in the company's direction, we fostered a culture of transparency and collaboration that enabled us to tackle challenges more effectively and adapt to the ever-changing business landscape. Moreover, this process encouraged a sense of ownership among employees, boosting their motivation, commitment, and overall job satisfaction. As a result, Electriq became a more resilient, innovative, and dynamic organization better equipped to navigate the complexities of the modern business world.

CREATING CULTURE

You don't create culture. You embody the culture that you want to set for your organization.

And as the leader and CEO, people look to you as an example of how to conduct yourself personally and professionally. You can help shepherd culture. But it's ultimately going to be the collective efforts of your entire team for shaping what that culture ends up being as a team. And so you can help shape it by hiring key team members in the correct positions that center around what you want the business to operate and feel like. But you can't take a top-down approach to culture.

If you have thriving and happy employees, you have a thriving company. And sure, you could have a flourishing company of unhappy employees, but in the long run, that's not sustainable. It will lead to burnout and high turnover.

None of these things are good for building a sustainable business for long-term growth. That is why making a culture where your employees thrive is crucial because it will make your overall business thrive and ultimately impact the bottom line. The more you invest in your team, the more you'll be able to either charge for the services or level up the product to charge a higher rate. You pay for what you get. And creating a culture of empowered teams goes beyond pay.

For most people, one of the most critical components of a job is pay because that impacts other portions of their life. It's also a way to express the value you think a team member is bringing. But there are so many other intangibles and things that a company should be considering, whether it's from HR support and services to other financial incentives like 401K to healthcare insurance, not only for your team members but also for their dependents.

But culture goes beyond benefits as well. There needs to be an overall tone of respect where it is clear the organization understands boundaries, has teams with thriving personal lives, and wants to make sure they are supported to be the best they can be, personally and professionally. Most importantly, there needs to be a culture of trust where management and executives believe their team members will do what they were hired to do.

All of these go into taking a more holistic approach to making your employees' lives better and easier, which in turn will make your company better.

You spend a good chunk of your week working at least forty or more hours, and so, of course, work affects you both personally and professionally. Listening, engaging, and encouraging your team to provide input and feedback on how the company treats its team members and what it's doing, in general, is one of the best ways to make your company people first.

And it's imperative to do so because if the company cares about the team, your team will have much more buy-in to the vision of what you're doing. You'll have much better retention of your team members as well. And the more ownership you can give your team over what they are doing, the better.

WHAT PEOPLE-FIRST ACTUALLY GETS YOU

It's more than just a statement. It needs to be an embedded philosophy. You can't just pay lip service to it—it must be a part of your and the company's DNA. There's nothing worse than paying lip service to being people-first, but your culture and policies are not.

To truly be people-first, the overall business posture needs to prioritize the well-being and satisfaction of employees over other considerations, such as profit maximization. The benefits are clear: improved productivity, increased employee satisfaction and retention, and better customer service. And it's good for a business's bottom line because it leads to a more motivated, dedicated, and efficient workforce.

One of the key benefits of a people-first culture is that it leads to improved productivity. When employees feel valued, supported, and empowered, they are more likely to be engaged and motivated to do their best. This can result in higher productivity levels, as employees are more likely to put in extra effort and work collaboratively to achieve common goals. Additionally, you can foster a sense of ownership and responsibility among teams, which can also contribute to improved productivity–since they own it, they care about it.

Perhaps most critical is that you aim to improve employee satisfaction and retention. The cost of losing a valued team member with deep institutional knowledge is higher than most companies take into account. When employees feel valued and supported, they are more likely to be happy and stay with the company longer. Additionally, satisfied employees are more likely to be loyal to the company and go above and beyond in their work, which can positively impact the overall success of the business.

And we can't forget about customer service. When team members feel valued and supported, they are more likely to be engaged and motivated in their work, which can translate into better service for customers and clients. Satisfied employees are also more likely to be empathetic and understanding of customer needs, which can help to build strong customer relationships and foster loyalty.

Improved productivity? Check. Increased employee retention? Check. Happy customers? Check.

RESEARCH BACKS THIS

A study published in the *Harvard Business Review* found that companies with a robust people-first culture had higher productivity levels and better financial performance than those with a weaker culture. Additionally, research from the University of California found that companies with a people-first culture had higher levels of employee satisfaction and lower turnover rates, which can benefit businesses. And there are far more. While not being profit-focused feels counterintuitive, we're finding it's better for business and leads to more profits!

Trends are already heading there, prompted by the pandemic. There is increasing emphasis on employee well-being and satisfaction in the workplace. In recent years, many companies have begun to focus on creating a positive, supportive, and engaging work environment for their employees, recognizing that this can have several benefits, including improved productivity and better financial performance.

There is a growing recognition of the importance of soft skills, such as communication, collaboration, and problem-solving, in the modern workforce. Many companies are now looking for employees with these skills, as they believe they are essential for success in today's fast-paced, complex business environment. By prioritizing developing these skills, businesses can create a more positive and productive work environment that ultimately leads to better financial performance.

And clearly, flexible and adaptable workplaces have become table stakes. But many companies recognize that these arrangements can benefit employees, as they can provide more control over their work-life balance and improve their well-being. By offering these options, businesses can create a more positive and productive work environment that ultimately leads to better financial performance.

All of this being said, we need to tread carefully. I've seen friends and colleagues take advantage of these newfound perks, and if the business doesn't have appropriate accountability checks and balances in place, it's a recipe for disaster.

TIME TO THINK DIFFERENT ABOUT BUSINESS

Legacy business management culture comes from a place of widgets and manufacturing. Productivity was about the output of products when America started its first business boom, and that thinking never really disappeared.

Now we are past the information economy and into a new playing field. We can no longer look at teams as widget-makers. They are thinkers. And all of us together form a circuit, and the structural integrity and efficiency of our connection make us power our industries.

In many ways, this is about going back to the basics. Treat people well. Make sure they are taken care of. And when you do that, everything else seems to fall into place.

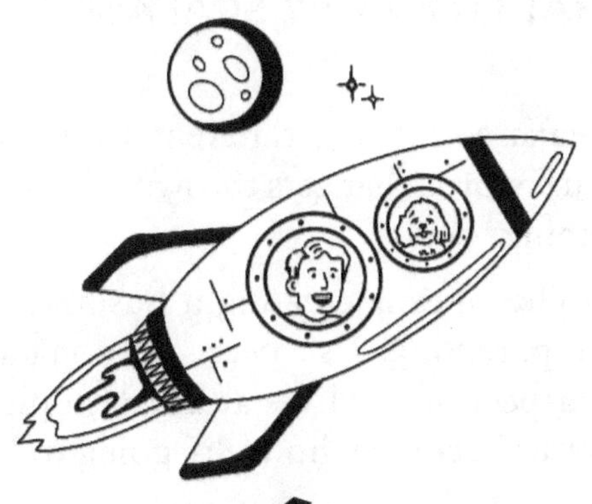

6

BUILD FOR SCALE

GROWING A BUSINESS IS ABOUT MORE THAN JUST RAIS-
ING MONEY. It most certainly is not about expanding as
quickly as possible at all costs.

I didn't exactly know that.

Fortunately, I navigated through this into a successful exit, but
I could've had a better handle on scalability before I pushed growth
into high gear. It is important to unpack what growing business entails–foundationally. Before the money, before the employees, and
before expanding into offices.

We will get into scalability in this chapter, but mainly from the
point of view of building a good foundation for scale. Entering the
space with a business designed for scale makes growing infinitely easier. And as a nice side effect, a scalable foundation is inherently more
resilient–something else that is needed during these uncertain times.

BUT FIRST, WHAT I MEAN BY SCALABILITY AND WHY IT MATTERS

Scalability means something different to everyone. It's one of those corporate buzzwords that gets thrown around and has, in some ways, lost its meaning.

For me, scalability means creating a business that can outgrow you. It's a lot like parenting, I suspect. We don't want our parents involved in every aspect of our lives at 25. At some point, they need to let us go and let us become who we're going to be.

Business leaders who create a scalable foundation have created a company that will outgrow them, outlive them, and become its own entity. So letting go of business operations is a lot like parents letting us go.

It isn't easy, and the longer it takes to build a scalable foundation that isn't reliant upon the founder, the longer business leaders are attached to the minutia of the business. We are only people. We can't be expected to manage, oversee, and control every conceivable aspect of our companies. And when we do, we constrain and sometimes strangle our businesses.

Founders can be a business's single largest bottleneck to growth.

So when I talk about scalability, I'm talking about building your business in a way that allows it the opportunity to grow and run itself.

So why is that important?

It enables businesses to grow and expand without being constrained by the limitations of their current systems and processes. To grow and expand without being constrained by its founder.

By building a scalable foundation, business leaders can create a company that can adapt and grow as needed and that has the potential to outlive and outgrow them. This allows them to focus on other business areas or step back from day-to-day operations.

It's about creating sustainable, long-term growth and success.

Because all of this isn't about you—it's about your business.

> *Test yourself – if you disappeared for a month, would your business as well?*

BUILDING FOR SCALE

I know this is a trap that almost every business in the service industry falls into because I fell into it. There is this notion that a single person will have multiple organizational roles. This is the "you wear many different hats" part of the job description. I suppose that fundamentally, that is unavoidable within start-ups, but forward-thinking entrepreneurs can avoid this by making their business as scalable as possible out of the gates.

A business's ability to scale is directly tied to healthy work culture. And that's because one person should not necessarily wear many hats. They should own their specific expertise and focus on that.

I learned that the hard way.

Our first hire was tasked with whatever immediate client work was lying around because we were trying to handle all of the SEO and content demand we had coming into the door. A process for workflow was utterly nonexistent. The "process" involved meeting the team member at the office and haphazardly walking her through what I was trying to accomplish and what we were working on. Then it was off to the races.

We didn't have 90% of our processes defined at that point either, as we were making it up on the fly, so there was only a little to onboard. But later, we had to develop a more refined onboarding process as we scaled.

Your business won't be built for scale from the get-go, but you should be laying the foundation over the first two years.

On my agency's journey, two years were painfully slow for me regarding growth. I had a difficult time taking market share. I'm impatient–I admit that. But I was limiting myself by not being set up for growth and scale. Early team members were on double duty. They were doing their role but also acting like project managers. I can't speak for them, but I'm guessing they weren't thrilled about it.

So we began to adapt to the need for scale and started institutionalizing processes necessary to undertake so we wouldn't accidentally kill ourselves.

We did several key things, but one of the most impactful was creating a client success management role for every brand we work with. They could take on the responsibility of being a brand manager and make sure the team was in sync with the client and that the client was happy with our deliverables and strategy. It created cohesiveness and strong attention to workflow detail. Now we could scale because each team member was only wearing one hat.

I wanted people to be focused on what they're good at, and it's very challenging to find a team member who can not only wear multiple hats but also want to do so. Even if they are excited about the multitudes of hats, they will inevitably be distracted and unable to invest themselves as heavily into one specific area completely. So that was a crucial part of adaption for us to manage that scale.

Another thing was for me to figure out how and what I could delegate and who I could elevate within the organization to allow us to continue to scale. We never had much success hiring senior-level positions from outside the company; frankly, I prefer to just promote from within. That way, I can be sure these team members are already familiar with our culture. I also found that people enjoy working at a business that promotes and provides upward mobility.

Team members with a history in the company are invested in what we are doing. As a business leader, I'm more comfortable and confident that they are willing to take on the challenge and look at the company as a byproduct of their own doing and creation. That is a critical part of the culture we've been able to manifest. This business is just as much theirs as it is mine.

We did it quickly and early on, and it worked out almost all the time and contributed to what would become a culture of ownership.

The rest of the team saw a place for them to grow within the organization, thrive both personally and professionally, and be valued members in building something from the ground up. With a culture like that, they have little incentive to look outside the organization, even if pay might be better elsewhere.

Another thing we did to manage and prepare for scale was creating an onboarding process for new team members. It took us a while to get there, but now we have about a week-long onboarding process where we have documents, training procedures, resource guides, and everything a new hire needs to feel comfortable in their new role and that they are a part of the team. It is engineered so that they feel confident, safe, prepared, and excited to become a part of Electriq. Too many organizations just throw new team members into the fire, hoping they'll find their way. And too many organizations go to the other extreme, where they grind down their team members with rigorous procedures and processes that inhibit growth rather than enable it. But that's not a pathway to success. It's not a positive experience. It's hard to be confident and happy that way. Unhappy team members also mean unhappy clients.

Having a remote workforce allows you to hire talented people from all over the world, but it makes it significantly harder to create a culture where everyone feels like they are a part of the same team. Our onboarding process goes to great lengths to immerse our new team members into the entire organization as quickly as possible to ensure they don't feel lost.

Now that we've built with scale in mind, we can hire multiple team members who are not adding revenue and do so without pain or urgency. We can do what we need to get them up to speed, train them effectively, and make sure they are set up for success.

ONBOARDING AND HIRING

The first iterations of our onboarding process were more about me initially spending one-on-one time with our new team members and helping walk them through what we did, our operations, and our goals and vision.

And that worked at first, but eventually, it got to a point where two main things happened.

One, when you're at forty to fifty team members, and I'm doing all of these other things that I need to do to continue to grow and operate the business, I just didn't have the time to continue to onboard all of these new team members in this one to one fashion that's not scalable. And also, as we brought on some other departments and started to specialize in more areas, someone other than me was the best person to give some of these onboarding training and sessions.

That started to come from the department heads once we brought those roles on. So the iteration for part one was a lot easier because I focused on getting these team members up to speed in a one-to-one fashion.

But then it became, how do I empower our department heads to build out their onboarding process? It evolved to a point where we now have our general onboarding, but then we have our department-specific onboarding. It's set up to be so thorough that you could never talk to the new team member - but we don't do this because it wouldn't be optimal.

Use a solution like Loom to record everything you do, from workflow processes to your actual work product deliverables. Every team member at Electriq has a Loom account and is encouraged to "record anything that they think could be useful for another team member to have as a resource" and then share it with our internal agency operations team.

It's to a point where we can hand new team members the onboarding documents, and they would be up to speed with the company culture and acquire all of the skills and knowledge to work at Electriq through our videos, resource guides, training, and certifications.

Part one is designed for every new team member, and part two is department specific. So again, more videos, more training, more certifications, and all of that took a lot of time to get to, but now that we're in this position, it's setting up our new team members for success and not causing us to reinvent the wheel on certain things that we know we don't need to.

This isn't to say we nailed it right out of the gate. We had some bumps in the road, especially in that in-between phase between phase one iteration of onboarding versus phase two, where we had one or two team members leave because they didn't feel like they had any idea what was going on nor how they could be successful in the role.

That was my wake-up call to hone in on how I could evolve our onboarding process to accommodate our new scale.

Because just like with onboarding a new client, that first week is crucial to ensure the relationship is set up for long-term success.

FOUNDER RESPONSIBILITIES

The founder's role in the organization is tough to define because it varies throughout the company's growth stages. But ultimately, I'd say the founder's role is to ensure that the company is not only successful but to define for the organization what success looks like so that everyone is marching to the same beat towards the same goal.

As a founder, you must organize and architect your company's vision.

That being said, it's more powerful and resonates better when as a founder, you look towards your team members to help inform that vision and ensure there's buy-in from everyone across the board.

Business is not a one-person ship. It's not a one-person captain with a hundred crew mates. This is a flat organization where everybody's input and insight are expected.

At the end of the day, as a founder, you're responsible for defining business success and achieving it.

HOW MY ROLE EVOLVED

Early on, my role in the business was everything. Outbound, salesperson, client success manager, advertising specialist, email/SMS specialist, Shopify guru, copywriter, UI/UX designer, office manager, accountant, and more.

Paperwork, payroll, licensing with the state, HR, health insurance, the list goes on and on. And let me tell you, I don't exactly miss some of these responsibilities.

Gradually, I started to transition some of these functions to other people. And really, how my role has evolved is that in the early days, I was doing everything. I was tactical hands-on keyboard. Then, it became more about educating others on how to do something, i.e., email marketing. Now, I'm not even involved. Other team members are tasked with the hands-on training of new team members for email marketing.

At first, delegating and empowering are essential, but still checking deliverables before they go out the door. But, over time, your team takes this over entirely. If I had to look at every client's email & SMS campaign before they went out, I'd be working 48 hours a day.

Now that I've offloaded many day-to-day responsibilities, I am focused on a long-term strategic vision of the company versus being more operational. Questions like, "What are we doing today?" or "How are we getting through X, Y, and Z?" are handled by our VP, Alissa. Combined with delegating accounting, taxes, HR, and more, I can be much more efficient because I can quickly check in on all aspects of the company with our department leaders while focusing a lot of my time and attention on continuing to make sure that we are at the pinnacle of technological and digital innovation.

Electriq 2.0 - My Removal from the Day-to-Day: I am primarily focused on three things at the agency: Weekly newsletter, tech partnerships, and business development. By bringing on a leader like Alissa, who is even better equipped than me to handle the day-to-day, I can stay at the forefront of the industry and distill it down into actionable takeaways for Electriq, which she then operationalizes within the agency. I was so busy before with client work and other tasks that I couldn't do this to the extent that I can now. We are a significantly more valuable agency, with me handling LESS day-to-day deliverables.

I aspire for it to turn into something where I've been able to delegate everything I am not the strongest. And I can focus all of my time, attention, and efforts on what I think we do best, which is content creation, education, the building out of templates and training procedures for our team, the architecting of the long-term vision of the company, the sales process with net new prospects to lay out the vision to them. Those are the areas I'm strongest in, not things like invoicing, handling client accounts, and receivables.

I aim to be more focused on how to build and sustain businesses in a different mindset and framework than has traditionally been done in the past.

It's an evolving journey, and I don't think it's one that ever ends.

AND WHAT HAPPENS WHEN YOU SCALE

Knowing when it's time to scale and if your business is even set up to scale is critical. If you're not ready, you will damage the baseline you've already built thus far.

Look at your day-to-day. Do you have your overall processes documented so that you can theoretically onboard a new team member without ever speaking to them? What happens when you bring on three to five new team members weekly? Will an ad hoc approach to onboarding work? Probably not.

Next, do you have the revenue and cash flow to justify such an investment?

There wasn't some specific moment where I said, "Oh, like, this is now my time to scale. Scale now!"

It came from an overwhelming demand from new businesses that we either had to scale or say no to. And I had always wanted to scale the business, grow it, and potentially exit. The hold-up for me to scale was that we bootstrapped.

If you're not a bootstrap company, it's different because you aren't beholden to revenue coming in the door. You're accountable to investor money and your burn rate. So if we had raised money, I would have scaled up sooner because then we would have been better positioned to handle the inbound demand once it started coming in.

But it was dictated by, okay, we made $100,000 this month. We only paid $50,000 in salary. Let's hire four new team members, continue scaling the team, and bring on new clients. I paid myself a nominal wage, and everything else returned to the business. The most I ever took in salary was $10,000/mo when we were nearing $500K in MRR.

In hindsight, the number one thing I learned is that the people who were great for your company in that very early-stage startup environment might not be the ones that are good for you at that 40-person to 50-person team member level.

And the biggest thing there is process orientation. And not saying that we're like some big corporate conglomerate, but as you get bigger, there are more defined processes. And so team members who really thrive in the unknown, wearing many different hats, jumping around, and just making everything happen in that 1-5, 1-10 employee range were great. Still, if they couldn't adapt what they were doing and turn it into a repeatable process, we ran into some issues.

The transition from individual contributor to manager can be challenging, and I learned that some team members don't want to be managers; they prefer to stay individual contributors. I learned this the hard way, but all you have to do is ASK.

I also learned that the first clients won't necessarily be the ones that are with you the entire time. As we continued working our way upmarket and improving our services, it became clear that we outgrew some of our clients.

For example, I used to be the CSM and the lead strategist for all our clients. Those day-one clients were paying us probably 1/20th of what new clients were paying us. And so as we got bigger and bigger and I couldn't do that anymore, it was a complex process to explain to clients that I couldn't continue to work with them 1:1, that we needed to charge more, and in some cases simply needed to stop working together and help them find a more suitable partner. It's essential to be transparent and open about this because it would've been highly unfair to their businesses to keep trying to service them when I knew we couldn't under the existing framework.

Our little business had grown up. And that transition could have gone a bit smoother. But at the same time, we couldn't continue to spread ourselves that thin because where we're at now is a powerful place where we only work with strategic fits, and we're not going to reach outside of our defined parameters and set ourselves up for failure.

Another key lesson I learned from scaling is that there is a business you should say no to. Even though you think, "Oh, it's incremental revenue," you can reinvest it.

Suppose it's not a good fit, whether because of personality, industry, or whatever. In that case, you're going to spend so much time dealing with all the bullshit and the back and forth with the client, and this-and-that, it's going to end up being such a time suck that it's going to take away from you crushing it for some of your other clients. Say yes to the wrong things too often, and you get pulled in so many different directions you lose your identity.

They could be critical pillars of your growth and a solid referral base.

Going back, I 100% would have built out more of a documented onboarding process from day one that we could have built upon versus our helter-skelter ad hoc onboarding for the first ten new team members we brought on.

Not necessarily have it as built and fleshed out as it has evolved to today, but still provide an excellent framework for our first team members that would empower them to think about what they would incorporate into an onboarding. Now, I ask every new team member once they're a few weeks past their onboarding what they would change or add to it to make it a better experience.

LONG-TERM PREPARATION FOR SCALING

Business leaders need to plan long-term for how they will adjust the way they think about business operationally, how to start, how to grow, and how to maintain one.

One is deciding to be a fully remote, hybrid remote, or in-person work environment. Communication is entirely different in a remote environment versus in person. You can grab somebody and chat for two minutes. You get that face-to-face human interaction. It's much more interpersonal and connected.

Now, remote first has its perks of you can work from wherever but it's a freelance gig economy more than anything and isn't the best environment for significantly larger companies.

So you have 120 employees as we have at DRINKS right now. How do you connect employee number one and employee number 120? When they live in different parts of the country, they don't work in the same department and yet are a part of this larger organization. Business leaders need to prepare for how they will address this because communication breakdowns come as a byproduct of being remote-first.

SCALABILITY ISN'T JUST A BUZZWORD

The foundations around building a scalable business are not new. But many companies seem to bind themselves in a scarcity mindset or allow business leaders to be bottlenecks to the business. The super-controlling business leader is part of a legacy mindset.

As the business world continues to be uncertain and as companies that thrive continue to focus on resiliency, scalability will become a core business foundation, no matter what the business is, even if you don't have visions of becoming a giant company. Building your business for scale inherently means building resiliency to its core. Something that can adapt and thrive even without your day-to-day involvement.

Scaling a business can be a big deal, and being ready for it is important. If you're not prepared, you risk damaging what you've already built. When considering whether it's time to scale, consider how you currently do things daily. Do you have documented processes that new team members can follow without guidance? Can you onboard multiple new employees quickly and efficiently? Do you have the money to justify expanding? It's also important to consider the type of clients you're working with and whether they are a good fit for your business. Don't be afraid to say no to clients that may not align with your values or goals. As you get bigger, having a solid team and a culture of communication and transparency is also important. All these factors can help make the scaling process go more smoothly.

A solid foundation, transparent processes, and a strong team are crucial to scale a business successfully. Everything else will fall into place.

7

IT TAKES A VILLAGE

IT'S TIME TO SHIFT OUR FOCUS FROM TRADITIONAL BUSI-NESS METRICS to building relationships and fostering a thriving company culture. This is what we mean when we talk about the Gen Z mindset. Relationships are the most critical metric in the business world–and arguably all aspects of the Gen Z point of view. With good relationships, everything else falls into place (those business metrics we all hold so near and dear).

By embracing a relationship-first mindset, businesses can create strategic partnerships that drive growth and benefit all parties involved.

The business landscape constantly changes and evolves, with new technologies and competition emerging daily. In this fast-paced and constantly evolving environment, having strong partnerships can provide a competitive advantage and open up new growth opportunities. You cannot and should not do this yourself.

At the outset, this means forming strategic relationships and partnerships outside your company. Doing so will allow you to share resources and knowledge and combine their strengths to achieve common goals. Additionally, prioritizing partnership-building relationships can foster trust, mutual respect, and a sense of community, creating a more positive work culture and a more motivated workforce.

In a world where success is not just about what you know but also about who you know, a relationship-first approach to partnership building is essential for businesses looking to thrive and succeed in the long term. But this partnership mindset doesn't end there.

The relationships-first approach applies to building internal teams in the same way it applies to external partnerships. A strong and cohesive internal team can be a significant competitive advantage for a business, fostering trust, collaboration, and a sense of shared purpose. When team members are treated as partners and not just employees, they are more likely to be engaged, motivated, and committed to the company's success.

Businesses can build internal teams that function like partners by creating a company culture that values relationships and encourages collaboration. So, how? Encourage open communication, create opportunities for cross-functional collaboration, and recognize the contributions of each team member. It also promotes a sense of belonging, inclusivity, and psychological safety, where team members feel comfortable sharing their ideas and opinions.

In short, building internal teams as partners requires a holistic relationship-building approach, where team members are valued, supported, and empowered to contribute to the company's success. By fostering a relationship-first mindset within the company, businesses can create a thriving culture that drives innovation, engagement, and success.

EMPOWERED TEAMS

There are so many examples of when things weren't working, and a team member or a collective group at Electriq was able to solve and brainstorm around the problem and how we could make it better.

We do believe that teamwork and collaboration are the keys to success. We've embraced this relationships-first mindset and prioritize communication, cooperation, and mutual support. This approach has led to a thriving culture of problem-solving and creativity, where team members are empowered to find solutions together rather than working in silos.

And I see this on a daily or weekly basis. There's so much collaboration, so many Slacks in all the different departments around. "Hey, has anyone ever come across this issue" or "Has anyone had a creative solution for this particular client's problem?"

Whether through Slack, cross-functional meetings, or informal chats, team members at Electriq are encouraged to share their ideas and expertise. This cross-pollination creates a wealth of creative solutions, a sense of community, and a shared purpose.

What sets Electriq apart is our ability to collaborate and empower one another, even in the face of challenges. Whether a tricky client problem or an internal issue, our team members are always willing to lend a hand and find solutions together. This approach has helped us overcome obstacles and created a dynamic and innovative work environment where everyone feels valued and supported.

And that is really what makes Electriq so unique, is the ability for us to collaborate and empower one another to solve problems when an individual might be siloed and frustrated about something or can't get it done. Our relationship-first approach has helped us to build a thriving business, and we're excited to continue to grow and evolve together.

TEAM & PARTNERSHIP ORIENTED

The winner-take-all approach is no longer sufficient in today's market, as businesses face increasing customer demands and the competition is becoming more fierce.

Taking a team and partner-oriented approach is essential because it allows businesses to leverage the strengths of others, thereby increasing their competitiveness. For example, no single firm can be an expert in everything or solve all problems with finite resources. By partnering with other companies that complement your strengths and offer best-in-class services or technology, businesses can create a flywheel effect that helps everyone grow.

Whether it's tech companies integrating with other complementary solutions in the marketplace or agencies specializing and aligning with other agencies in areas they don't cover, it just makes good business sense to go deep in a specific area or areas and let the rest get handled by those with the expertise or technological capabilities.

Because even from a services standpoint, you can't be an expert in everything. And on the tech side, you have finite development resources, so you can only be a solution for some things. Going very deep into these particular services or focusing on a specific area as a technology solution, you can see this flywheel effect where you're supporting and helping each other grow.

Partnerships also allow businesses to pool resources, knowledge, and expertise, increasing innovation and growth potential. By working together, companies can create solutions that would not be possible otherwise. This kind of collaboration helps build stronger, more resilient companies better equipped to succeed in the long run.

And let's face it, out of all the business metrics we should look at; resilience is top of the list.

Partnerships are the #1 reason for Electriq's growth, success, and staying power.

MENTORSHIP

A key way to build and foster relationships is through mentorship. Through mentorship, business leaders and entrepreneurs can gain valuable insights and advice to help them avoid common mistakes and grow their companies more effectively.

It has been super important not only for me in getting Electriq off the ground and running but also for the ability to bounce ideas off somebody and get advice. It can help you avoid some obvious mistakes without making them yourself.

Mentorship provides a safe space to confide in someone they trust, get constructive feedback, and receive guidance on the best action. This type of support can be precious during the early stages of starting a business when the stakes are high and there are many unknowns. But it's also important as the business matures and the needs and stakes change over time.

I recommend that anybody embarking upon their entrepreneurial journey find a couple of close advisors and mentors they can rely on. I go out of my way to try and provide mentorship where I can because I know how invaluable it was to me and still is to me on my evolving journey. I've made lifelong friends from it as well!

In addition to supporting individual entrepreneurs, mentorship can be a valuable tool for building solid and resilient teams. By lifting team members through the organization, businesses can create a culture of growth and development that helps employees feel invested in the company and its success. This can lead to higher levels of engagement and loyalty, reducing the costs associated with employee turnover.

Within your organization, make it a priority to ensure every team member has some aspect of mentorship baked into their experience. Being able to lift our team members through the organization in terms of promotion engendered a lot of good faith within the company. Still, it also makes sense for your business to grow and scale effectively. Also, hiring senior team members into an existing organization and having them gel culturally while not bringing any of their bad habits or preconceived notions can be challenging.

Once you start to get those trusted team members in place, they become a part of the organization and family, and it's just so much easier and more fun to work with people you know and enjoy working with. You would prefer to have somebody on your team for two years versus having somebody on your team for three months. So, the ability to mentor junior team members into larger roles and help them grow both professionally and personally not only incentivizes them to stay, but the continuity of your team makes you a better company. Also, it's super expensive to rehire!

Mentorship is also something employees look for, and at Electriq was expressed to me as a desire in our feedback process when we needed to have a more formal approach.

A Caveat to Advice and Mentorship: With mentorship, just because you bounce ideas off someone or get advice doesn't mean you need to always act on it. There's nuance to everything. Getting advice from a mentor can help you avoid some obvious mistakes without having to make them yourself or fast-track you on the path to success.

INTERNAL PARTNER BUY-IN

Another thing that worked very well regarding a partner-oriented approach is ensuring the entire team is aligned with how important partnerships are to your organization. If you don't have buy-in from the rest of your team, especially when you start scaling and have a lot of employees, you won't see the same results we saw in the early days.

As Electriq grew, our partnership efforts started to falter a bit. This was my fault because I knew how vital our tech and agency partnerships were to the business, but I wasn't communicating clearly to the team. So, I started overemphasizing the importance of partnerships to our team, showcasing how they helped the business. And once they saw that, I got way more buy-in because it is way more powerful to tell somebody something and give them the why and context around it.

Depending on the situation, you can give some context for some things. Sometimes the minutiae could be more critical and distract the team member. But I found it a lot easier to get buy-in from the team when they know the why behind their actions.

WHEN THINGS WEREN'T WORKING – THE IMPORTANCE OF DEEP PARTNERSHIPS

Challenges or problems with tech partners revealed one of the most significant benefits of strong and deep relationships. So many times, we've run into issues with a product or an integration between the two products we use. And maybe it's not even an issue. It could be something where we see there could be an opportunity for it to do better or some unique use case or feature that we'd like to roll out with a client.

Our deep tech partnerships allow us to go to somebody and say that this is a priority or something with much potential.

Can we help you and work with you on making this a reality? We can help on the services side and test into customers, and the tech partner can support us from a development standpoint.

And that's been invaluable because Electriq gets to be a part of all the beta initiatives with the top Shopify technology partners, making us more informed and on the cutting edge of new technology, translating into results for our clients.

This isn't a one-sided relationship, either. For tech partners, agencies like Electriq provide access to 50+ clients, give free product ideas and feedback, and act as an external sales force and client success manager. All of our tech partner's data shows that clients who work with an agency have greater product adoption and higher retention rates than those who don't.

So the complexities and challenges around building strong external strategic partnerships helped all parties better serve the marketplace. The journey is half the point!

Technology partners are the number one source of new business for Electriq this year.

And the impact doesn't stop at referrals. It helps build trust with a prospect, showing credibility from a third-party source who has way more awareness than you do, instantly allowing you a seat at the table and making you much more competitive in the eyes of the prospect. It's why our certifications, such as Shopify Plus Certified, Klaviyo Elite, Rebuy Gold, Okendo Platinum, Attentive Pioneer, and Recharge Agency Partner of the Year are so necessary.

THE LEGACY APPROACH: SILOS

Business leaders who choose to isolate themselves rather than form partnerships put themselves at a disadvantage. During uncertain times, such a competitive mindset can leave them feeling isolated and unable to collaborate with others in their industry.

Without the support of trusted partners, it becomes much more challenging to weather difficult times. This can lead to a sense of being stuck in an echo chamber, where the leader becomes increasingly out of touch with what's happening in the larger ecosystem.

On the other hand, having strong partnerships with tech partners, other agencies, and business leaders in the industry creates a much more robust and reliable environment. By sharing insights and supporting each other, partners can help overcome challenges, generate new ideas, and rise together.

This collaborative approach can help businesses weather tough times and emerge even stronger. And by forming solid partnerships and mentorship relationships, business leaders can help prevent isolation and stay connected to the broader business community.

One of the best things in our partner-oriented approach that we've taken is finding a mutual client or mutual success story that you can then build off of. So we found a lot of new tech partners and new agency partners. That way, where we have one customer overlap, we see great results and then take that out. Then we take that out to the market and also start helping each other co-sell.

And so it's a lot more work to start entirely from scratch. But if you get that first one, really focus on making that one great. Make a case study and use it in your business development efforts.

Using the marketplace as an ecosystem of support rather than a competitive jungle goes a long way.

A Note about "Competitors" in the Traditional Sense: Some of my closest friends in the industry and those I go to for advice are from "competitors" that provide almost the same services as we do. This ecosystem is enormous, and there is no shortage of opportunity for all of us. We'll be far better off if we support and lift each other up! This is NOT Coke vs Pepsi.

8
EXIT STRATEGY

IT WASN'T THAT MANY YEARS AGO WHEN I FIRED UP some freelance work for extra cash during college. But it feels like a lifetime ago. In just a few years, I went from working on my laptop in a coffee shop to jet-setting worldwide to broker strategic partnerships with some of the largest brands in my industry. Through the many pitfalls and victories, it has become clear that business is every bit about the journey as it is the destination.

And when I started Electriq, it could only be about the journey. I had absolutely no idea what the destination was. Nor could I have conceived it would land where it did.

We're going to look at Electriq's destination in this chapter. We witnessed its journey from the coffee shop to the windowless dungeon office, meteoric growth, pivot into specialization, and development of a Gen Z-oriented culture. Now we'll cover Electriq's role as a business driver for an alcohol technology company. And we'll see how the perfect fit can move mountains when stars align or when there is lightning in a bottle.

So I want to unpack what happened when DRINKS acquired Electriq. We can review the valuable lessons I learned about entrepreneurship, leadership, and building a solid team. We'll also touch on the many challenges I faced and the difficult decisions I had to make.

WAS ACQUISITION THE PLAN ALL ALONG?

Ultimately, I always knew I wanted to sell Electriq, but I didn't know how or when that would happen. I didn't realize how quickly it would happen, the size we would need to be, or the scale. I didn't know much about the process or realities of selling a business. I mean, this was the first time I had even started one!

As an aspiring entrepreneur, I've always been motivated by the challenge of building and growing a business. It's about the journey—the process of building something, watching it grow, and seeing it succeed. While I love marketing, I knew that I didn't want to be running a marketing agency for the rest of my life. I'm always looking for new challenges and opportunities to learn and grow.

As Electriq grew and scaled, the acquisition idea became more real and tangible. It wasn't just a far-off dream but a real possibility we needed to plan for and work towards. I began to focus on building systems and processes that would allow the business to run without me, as I knew that would be a key factor in attracting a buyer.

As a result, I quickly learned the importance of creating a sustainable and scalable business model that can function independently of its founder. It became clear that building a successful business is not just about the founder's vision but about creating a team and culture that can continue to grow and thrive even if the founder is no longer involved.

I also learned how important it was to find the right buyer at the right time, which also included a fair amount of luck. While I always knew that acquisition was the end goal for Electriq, I also knew that it was important to wait for the right opportunity and partner. Selling to the wrong company or at the wrong time could have negative consequences, such as losing our culture or not realizing the total potential value of the company.

As a first-time business owner, I was thrilled when multiple parties began to inquire about acquiring Electriq. It was exciting to think that our hard work and success had attracted the attention of potential buyers. However, as things progressed, I realized that only some inquiries were worth pursuing. Some parties wanted to kick the tires or get a feel for the market, while others were genuinely interested in exploring a potential acquisition.

It's imperative as a business owner not to get ahead of yourself and start spending too much of your time on acquisition opportunities and not enough on your business. It was difficult for me not to get overly excited about the acquisition inquiries and start daydreaming about what things could be like. Still, you mustn't take your eye off the prize and continue to execute at a high level for your business.

During the exploratory phase, it's important to have a strong sense of what you're looking for in a potential buyer and to differentiate between serious inquiries and those simply wasting your time. You need to balance pursuing possible deals and staying within reach of yourself. It's a delicate dance that requires a lot of patience and focus, but finding the right buyer and getting the best possible deal for your business is essential. If an acquirer is serious, they'll ensure you know it.

IT WAS TIME TO VIEW BUSINESS DIFFERENTLY

I used to have a mindset that business was all about putting in long hours and brute-forcing your way through challenges. While hard work is undoubtedly important, I realized that as an entrepreneur, my role shifted over time. I needed to focus on empowering my team to be successful rather than trying to do everything myself.

Scaling a company requires collaboration and teamwork. The owner's responsible for finding team members whose personal goals align with the business objectives and empowering them to achieve both. This helps create a positive environment where everyone benefits and the organization thrives.

Collaboration and teamwork are essential to achieving success.

I used to think it was a buzzword in corporate culture to "collaborate." And maybe it is in organizations with legacy thinking. But for me, authentically building a collaborative culture was mandatory. I couldn't do this on my own. I needed to build a team with people I trusted and who trusted me. I needed to empower them to lift the agency without me. By giving each team member the space to achieve their goals while working towards our shared objectives, the organization thrived and truly was a positive environment that benefited everyone.

Previously, I viewed business as something akin to a traditional corporate environment where you show up, do your job, work hard, and do it primarily for monetary gain. However, I needed to shift my thinking if I was going to build Electriq into a viable resource for another company. There is so much more to business than that. It's about solving problems, focusing on the proper work, building valuable experts, trusting the teams you make to carry the organization, and doing things purposefully.

Shifting my mindset to focus on the bigger picture of building a successful company was critical to Electriq's journey. It meant recognizing that building a company was more than working hard for financial gain. It required focusing on problem-solving, prioritizing important work, developing valuable expertise, building a trustworthy team, and working purposefully. This change in mindset allowed me to create an organization that was successful and attractive to potential buyers. By understanding the importance of collaboration and team empowerment, I was able to build a company that could thrive even without my direct involvement.

HOW DID I DETERMINE WHEN AND WHO?

The decision to sell a company is always a challenging one. For me, it was a matter of determining whether the sale was a good strategy for Electriq and me. After analyzing the financials, it became clear that an acquisition was the best option, as it would de-risk what had been built up until that point and provide me with lifelong financial stability—even more importantly, the opportunity to learn and try new challenges.

However, choosing the right buyer was just as important. I didn't want to be acquired by someone who would treat us as a mere cog in the wheel. DRINKS was the perfect fit as a software company entering into a new space where our Shopify expertise and ecosystem accreditations would instantly catapult them to a new level, and the sum of our parts would be greater than the whole. I also knew them, understood them, and hypothesized that the goals and cultures would fit together well.

Once I determined that the sale was a good strategy for the company, I needed to be selfish and see whether it made sense for me. If Electriq had stopped growing and just maintained its current P&L, it would have taken me three to four years to distribute the same amount of cash that the acquisition offered upfront while not giving me any additional equity upside in a thriving tech business at the forefront of an entire vertical. The time value of money equation weighed heavily towards selling, as well as incurring capital gains vs. ordinary income tax and getting that money up front, still sharing in the upside of the larger entity, and de-risking what had been built up until that point made it an obvious yes for me.

When it came to choosing and selecting the buyer, it came down to whether it was a good fit for the agency and myself. I knew DRINKS was a good fit. I was going to dive in and learn a different aspect of the ecommerce industry, which is something I was looking for—the ability to roll up my sleeves again and try new and differing challenges. And I could see why we were so valuable and necessary for them in terms of helping them get to the next level along their journey.

I wanted to avoid getting acquired by somebody where I'd just be a cog in the wheel and then get churned out after a year or two, post-earn-out, or whatever. It came down to whether the buyer was a good fit, whether I would be personally interested in it, whether Electriq was indeed a value add for them, and whether I was a value add for them.

The acquisition plugged me into many new relationships within the Shopify ecosystem that I wouldn't have had access to before as one of the hundreds of Plus agencies. We're also working with clients we would never have had access to. It was a match made in heaven in that sense, how we can complement each other's strengths and weaknesses in their beverage alcohol background and expertise and our Shopify background and expertise. They also up-leveled us professionally, walking us into Fortune 500 relationships. At the same time, we helped flatten their organization a bit and add some Gen Z fun to it!

WHAT I WISH I KNEW

Looking back, I wish I had known before the acquisition process started that it would go slower than I expected, especially with everyone working remotely across different time zones. There were holidays, and sometimes days would go by with very little progress being made. This was the most frustrating part because I had already mentally shifted my focus to the new opportunity and what we could accomplish together after the merger.

I had gotten ahead of myself regarding timing and thought it would only take about 30 days since it was a clear-cut deal. However, things dragged on, and I wanted the process to wrap up so I could move on and focus on the more considerable opportunity. I remember feeling anxious and impatient because I had already started planning the next steps in my mind.

This experience taught me that the acquisition process can be lengthy, complicated, and unpredictable and that it's crucial to have patience and remain focused on the business during this time. As an entrepreneur, it's essential to be adaptable and ready for unexpected challenges that may arise during an acquisition. Deals can and likely will fall through; you can't weaken your business because of it.

Knowing how long the acquisition process can take, I would have invested less mental energy and time exploring the joint opportunity. I would have been disappointed if the acquisition didn't go through, and it would have been a struggle for me. However, it's essential to recognize that these delays and setbacks are a part of the process, and it's crucial to remain patient and focused on the larger goal.

Now that the acquisition is complete and some time has passed, I can look back and think of some takeaways and lessons learned.

For example, it has become increasingly clear that there needs to be more understanding among new team members about the larger organization and the opportunities that come with it. While the acquisition was an excellent opportunity for both companies, ensuring everyone on the team is on the same page about the organization's goals and mission is essential.

The lack of understanding is particularly acute among new team members who may not have been present during the acquisition process. They may not understand why Electriq was acquired, the parent company's goals and ambitions, or that we were once separate companies.

To address this issue, we're continually developing onboarding programs that get new team members up to speed on the entire organization, including its history, goals, and opportunities. We now integrate new team members fully into business, regardless of the team they're joining. This approach ensures everyone is on the same page, increasing the likelihood of success across the organization.

Another critical learning about integrating the two teams post-sale is that we could have been quicker. It's more beneficial to be fully integrated instead of operating as separate entities. There was a fair amount of overlap, and we could have leveraged each other's expertise in certain areas. We're now doing that effectively but could've done it even quicker.

Fast forward to today, when people are willing to hop in and help out even if it doesn't necessarily fit within their job title or description. Team members are eager to assist in other areas where they can add value, regardless of whether they are part of the DRINKS or Electriq team.

Despite having different business units, we emphasize that we are all one team. It's essential to be cross-collaborative and share where possible to improve efficiencies and make everyone's lives easier. If we were to do it again, we would integrate the teams more quickly to mesh the culture and get everyone on the same page ASAP. This approach would also free up bandwidth and resources.

LOOKING BACK

My age and Gen Z qualities played a significant role in this journey. I approached it with a blank slate and felt free NOT to follow the standard norm or paradigm other agencies and organizations created.

This allowed us to create a unique culture of autonomy and creativity that couldn't be easily replicated elsewhere. Our age and Gen Z qualities led to an environment where we worked hard and valued everyone's opinion, regardless of their seniority.

We didn't want to hire robots and expected all team members to contribute to the company's vision. Creating a healthy, thriving environment where employees are invested in the organization's mission is essential for a successful company. We were able to generate this kind of culture at Electriq.

Integrating my role into the new structure of DRINKS is still an evolving process because we were acquired to open a new division within the organization. They had never had a Shopify app before and needed to be more familiar and experienced with the Shopify ecosystem. So, we don't have all the pieces in place that would be needed at a pure Shopify app company, such as tech and agency partnerships, all the sales team members, all the customer support, etc. But it's super exciting to jump in, be valued, and build that from the ground up.

My role, in some ways, hasn't changed a lot. I still wear many hats, including overseeing the day-to-day agency operations. And my role is constantly evolving in this new structure, which is also why I enjoy the opportunity. I'm not pigeonholed and defined into a narrow scope, which would be boring and limiting.

But ultimately, when I look back, one of the biggest bullets we dodged was going through an acquisition that wasn't the right fit for us, just for financial gain. There were opportunities for an agency rollup, but that would have compromised our culture and turned us into "doers" rather than leveraging our unique strengths. The wrong partner or deal structure could have substantially impacted our business today, so I'm glad we could avoid that.

My biggest takeaway from this journey of building and selling a business is that success relies on your team more than anything else. As an individual contributor, you can only do so much. To build an acquirable company, you must create an organization that allows others to thrive, grow, and achieve their goals.

With any business, managing people and being authentic and genuine is critical to achieving mutual goals that benefit everyone. This lesson will help me succeed in any vertical or industry, as it ultimately comes down to the people.

WHAT'S NEXT

My main focus is on the DRINKS.com opportunity, specifically the DRINKS App on Shopify, which enables alcohol commerce across the entire United States on the Shopify platform. I'm also highly focused on unlocking the 4th tier opportunity with Shopify, where we can turn any merchant into an alcohol merchant.

Separately, in the background over the last 18 months, my brother and I have been building a product in the HR space called SCALIS. It's a dual-sided ATS/job board system incorporating a patent-pending matching algorithm and anonymization AI software. I've been funding the project until now, and as of the release of this book should be wrapping up our seed round.

Ideally, I want to see DRINKS through acquisition and stay on to help transition to the acquiring company. Then, I plan to transition into a role at SCALIS and achieve a successful exit for the third time. It's good to set big goals, right?! :)

In the meantime, I'm also focusing on building my brand and creating more content. Having an audience is essential today, and it can lead to more connections and opportunities that wouldn't have been possible otherwise. Beyond that, I want to empower others in a similar situation to me four years ago to go out and do it! These are my main priorities at the moment.

SHOULD YOU CONSIDER AN ACQUISITION STRATEGY

Acquisition is something that founders should consider for multiple reasons, depending on the goal behind the acquisition. Are you looking to scale up and make a more significant exit with your next company? Or are you seeking liquidity to exit your current engagement? The founder's objectives dictate whether an acquisition is worth considering, and inherent benefits and risks depend on the goal.

Working with a larger entity can provide additional resources if you consider an acquisition to continue growing and scaling your business and have an earn-out or similar incentive. However, the downside is that you may have less control over the company than before, reducing your autonomy. It can be challenging for an entrepreneur who has been running their own business to become part of a larger organization where they are not the final decision-maker, which can lead to issues.

If this is your direction, you must make your company more valuable to an acquirer. Do this by institutionalizing your processes and the secret sauce that your company brings. This means setting up your company so that anyone can train themselves on your procedures, turn into a team member, and contribute towards the business goals without you needing to be there daily. Your company won't be as valuable if it can't run without you, and it will require you to be tethered to it.

Second, focus on increasing your revenue, mainly monthly recurring revenue. The more guaranteed and contractual revenue, the more valuable your company will be. For instance, if you're a web development agency that only does one-time projects, you won't be as valuable as an email marketing agency that earns the same revenue but on annual or monthly retainer contracts. That's because guaranteed income that's more predictable is coming through the door.

Entrepreneurs should consider their goals when starting a company. Some entrepreneurs may not necessarily think about an exit plan, but they should consider what they want to achieve with their business. For instance, they may want to freelance and have control over their work schedule, or they may want to scale and grow their business into a 20 or 25-person lifestyle company.

If you can't define what success looks like, how is your team supposed to know what they are working towards? Maybe it's an outsized exit, taking the company public, or having a more meaningful work product they can control. While some of these goals may require an exit plan, not all do.

While it's good to be aware of your exit strategy, prioritizing it over everything else could ultimately hurt the business. Suppose entrepreneurs think about the exit plan from the beginning. In that case, they may be premature and overlook other important aspects of building a successful company, potentially doing things that short-term increase value but long-term are detrimental.

Building the Business for Acquisition

If you're considering acquisition as your exit strategy, you need to build your business in a way that allows it to run independently without you being there. This is especially important if you plan on staying with something other than the acquiring company long-term.

To do this, you must establish systems and processes that give the company value and make it a thriving entity. Your business needs to operate without your daily involvement. Although, initially, you may need to be involved in everything, over time, you must remove yourself from the company's day-to-day operations as much as possible. This will ensure that it's a thriving entity that can survive and thrive without you being at the helm every day.

Also, it's essential to be clear with the acquirer early on that your business's culture makes it attractive to them. It was crucial for me and my team to ensure that our culture would be maintained once the acquisition was completed. Additionally, it's important to consider taking some aspects of the acquiring company's culture and embedding them into your own, improving both organizations.

Both teams must be aligned on the overarching opportunity and willing to adapt and change to improve the organization. This requires transparency and the ability to express and sell the opportunity presented by merging both organizations. You don't want team members to be protective or resistant to change. Therefore, it's vital to have a team open to change and willing to embrace the new opportunities that come with an acquisition.

There are many factors to consider before selling a business, but ultimately, the key question is, will you be happy with the decision? It was also important to consider if I would be satisfied if I turned down the acquisition opportunity and another one didn't come up in the near future. The answer to both questions was a definite yes and no, respectively. The deal structure and opportunity with the acquiring company made sense, and I could see where I would fit in and provide value. From a financial standpoint, it made sense to capitalize on the opportunity and pull out money from the business rather than wait three to four years at a higher tax rate.

Now, I can focus on new and different opportunities where I can learn and grow.

REFERENCES

SOURCES

Ed O'Boyle, "4 Things Gen Z and Millennials Expect From Their Workplace," Gallup, March 30, 2017, retrieved at https://www.gallup.com/workplace/336275/things-gen-millennials-expect-workplace.aspx

"Happy workers are 13% more productive," Oxford, October 24, 2019, retrieved at https://www.ox.ac.uk/news/2019-10-24-happy-workers-are-13-more-productive

Shane McFeely and Ben Wigert, "This Fixable Problem Costs U.S. Businesses $1 Trillion," Gallup, March 13, 2019, retrieved at https://www.gallup.com/workplace/247391/fixable-problem-costs-businesses-trillion.aspx

"Gartner Says U.S. Total Annual Employee Turnover Will Likely Jump by Nearly 20% From the Prepandemic Annual Average," Gartner, April 28, 2022, retrieved at https://www.gartner.com/en/newsroom/04-28-2022-gartner-says-us-total-annual-employee-turnover-will-likely-jump-by-nearly-twenty-percent-from-the-prepandemic-annual-average

"Majority of Workers Who Quit A Job In 2021 Cite Low Pay, No Opportunities for Advancement, Feeling Disrespected," Pew Research Center, March 8, 2022, retrieved at https://www.pewresearch.org/fact-tank/2022/03/09/majority-of-workers-who-quit-a-job-in-2021-cite-low-pay-no-opportunities-for-advancement-feeling-disrespected/ft_2022-03-09_greatresignation_01/

Cara Salpini, "These traditional brands are shifting to a DTC model. Here's How," RetailDive, November 11, 2021, retrieved at https://www.retaildive.com/news/these-traditional-brands-are-shifting-to-a-dtc-model-heres-how/607646/

Tom Treanor, "How CPG Brands Are Using DTC To Stay Competitive," Forbes, October 8, 2020, retrieved at https://www.forbes.com/sites/forbes-communicationscouncil/2020/10/08/how-cpg-brands-are-using-dtc-to-stay-competitive/?sh=5c258ebc4fca

Michael Redbord, "The Hard Truth About Acquisition Costs (and How Your Customers Can Save You," Hubspot, August 2, 2023, retrieved at https://blog.hubspot.com/service/customer-acquisition-study

Neel Desai, "How is CAC Changing Over Time," Profitwell, August 14, 2023, retrieved at https://www.profitwell.com/recur/all/how-is-cac-changing-over-time

Nicholas Bloom, Hites Ahir, and Davide Furceri, "Visualizing the Rise of Global Economic Uncertainty," Harvard Business Review, September 29, 2022, retrieved at https://hbr.org/2022/09/visualizing-the-rise-of-global-economic-uncertainty

Denise Lee Yohn, "Company Culture Is Everyone's Responsibility," Harvard Business Review, February 8, 2021, retrieved at https://hbr.org/2021/02/company-culture-is-everyones-responsibility

"The USC Annenberg Relevance Report," USC Annenberg, November 1, 2022, retrieved at https://annenberg.usc.edu/research/center-public-relations/relevance-report#:~:text=The%20USC%20Annenberg%20Relevance%20Report&text=The%20book%20features%20contributions%20from,members%2C%20academics%20and%20student%20contributors

PARTNERS, TOOLS, AND BRANDS

Electriq: Brandon's Retention as a Service Shopify Plus Marketing Agency: https://www.electriqmarketing.com/.

DRINKS: technology company that powers digital commerce for the U.S. alcohol market and Electriq's parent company, https://www.drinks.com/.

Shopify: business commerce platform with an ecosystem of tools that help grow businesses online, https://www.shopify.com/.

Klaviyo: intelligent marketing automation platform focusd on omnichannel messaging for customers, powered by their data, https://www.klaviyo.com/.

Attentive: comprehensive personalzied text messaging solution, https://www.attentive.com/

TESTIMONIALS

"In all my years of partnerships, both agency side and tech side, I've never seen an agency rise from virtual anonymity to market leader as quickly as Electriq. Brandon possesses a natural curiosity that leads him to push the boundaries of ecommerce marketing and innovate. He's one of the most intelligent, ambitious, and driven business leaders I've had the opportunity to work with. It is a privilege to call him a partner and a friend."

\- Rachel Tyers, Co-Founder @ Nacelle & SVP of
Partnerships & Marketing @ Okendo

"Brandon has been one of the most innovative leaders in the space for the past four years. Brandon has always found a way to drive value at the intersection of commerce. Breaking out on the scene with the wedge of GenZ branding to building lasting relationships across the brand, agency, and tech players in the space, he's constantly hustling to help startups build the next great brand."

\- Jeremy Horowitz, Sr. Manager Partner
Marketing at Gorgias

"I've worked with Brandon for three years as a partner since the early days of Electriq. They've been one of our most valuable partners through referral agreements, supporting our mutual clients, and as a thought leader at our largest conferences. What's unique about Brandon and Electriq is that they are constantly innovating and are almost always one of the earliest adopters of new technologies and playbooks. Brandon has been instrumental in helping us enable hundreds of ecommerce agencies in "retention services" around our platform."

\- Billy McClennan, Director of Agency &
Technology Partnerships

"Electriq is one of the crown jewels in Klaviyo's partner program. Electriq is one of only 24 Elite partners out of over 12,000 partners in Klaviyo's partner program and rose to this status faster than any agency in our program. The secret to their success is their ability to incorporate the entire Shopify ecosystem and create a seamless email and SMS strategy. Their team gets the most out of loyalty, review, CS, post-purchase survey, quiz, and many other tech partners in their retention strategy. Electriq's clients grow faster and more sustainably than other brands that I have observed. Rest assured, if you are working with Electriq, you're in good hands."

- Dan Deren, Senior Partner
Manager at Klaviyo

"Electriq's growth has been impressive to watch and something we saw coming. Brandon has put together a very talented team that understands the full scope of what brands need and implements a profit-driving system - not a series of fragmented solutions or individual strategies. In this next chapter of commerce, I think this is what brands need, and they're just getting started."

- Tyler Prete, Manager of
Strategic Partnerships at Klaviyo

"The most impressive thing about Electriq is how quickly and sustainably it grew over its first few years. I believe Electriq first came to Klaviyo in early 2021 and, by mid-2022, was in the top handful of agency partners (out of 6,500+ agencies). So many agencies get it wrong - whether it's pricing, philosophy, or not getting into a niche and doing it well. Brandon very intentionally built Electriq with a clear ICP, process, and brand that delivers consistent results. Electriq picked a lane and dominated it. The clear vision and intentionality behind the company have catapulted not only Electriq but dozens of brands into exponential growth that has changed the game of eComm for an entire vertical. I can't wait to see what Brandon touches next and inevitably quadruples in the first six months."

- Leigh Fernandez, Sales Manager at Klaviyo

"Brandon has been an indispensable advisor and a genuine friend to our e-commerce SaaS company. His deep expertise in DTC customer retention, LTV, email, and SMS marketing has been instrumental in guiding our product's early development and fostering growth. In addition to his technical acumen, Brandon possesses a vast understanding of entrepreneurship and business expansion, all while maintaining a sincere warmth and kindness that sets him apart as an extraordinary mentor and ally throughout our journey. I am truly grateful for his unwavering support and friendship."

- Emilio Di Marco, Founder at Aument.io

"Brandon has been at the forefront of creating a strong retention strategy for brands. He's been instrumental in stitching together data sent from various apps and using that data to trigger more sophisticated automations within Klaviyo. There are probably only a few agencies doing this today, and Electriq is clearly leading the pack."

- Chathri Ali, VP of Growth at OceanX &
Former COO at Recharge

ACKNOWLEDGMENTS

I would like to thank my mother for dealing with my craziness and supporting me over the past 26 years in all my pursuits. I have not made things easy, and the highs and lows of entrepreneurship ring very accurate with me, but in the end, she always has my back.

I'd also like to thank Zac Brandenberg, my longtime mentor, who was paramount in helping me with everything from the backend operations of a business to thinking through how to create a thriving organization with institutionalized operations and knowledge that are not solely reliant upon me.

To my younger brother, Parker, I may have written the first book, but I'm confident that I will be looking up to you in the not-so-distant future.

I would not have been able to write this book without the guidance, support, and vision of my editor and longtime communications strategist, Mark Havenner, whom I look forward to embarking on many more projects together.